Global Terrorism and New Media

Global Terrorism and New Media carefully examines the content of terrorist websites and extremist television programming to provide a comprehensive look at how terrorist groups use new media today.

Based partly on a content analysis of discussion boards and forums, the authors share their findings on how terrorism 1.0 is migrating to 2.0 where the interactive nature of new media is used to build virtual organization and community. Although the creative use of social networking tools such as Facebook may advance the reach of terrorist groups, the impact of their use of new media remains uncertain. The book pays particular attention to terrorist media efforts directed at women and children, which are evidence of the long-term strategy that some terrorist organizations have adopted, and the relationship between terrorists' media presence and actual terrorist activity. This volume also looks at the future of terrorism online and analyzes lessons learned from counterterrorism strategies.

This book will be of much interest to students of terrorism studies, media and communication studies, security studies and political science.

Philip Seib is Professor of Journalism and Public Diplomacy, Professor of International Relations, and Director of the Center on Public Diplomacy at the University of Southern California.

Dana M. Janbek is Assistant Professor at the Department of Communication at Lasell College.

Media, War and Security

Series Editors: Andrew Hoskins, University of Warwick, and
Oliver Boyd-Barrett, Bowling Green State University

This series interrogates and illuminates the mutually shaping relationship between
war and media as transformative of contemporary society, politics and culture.

Global Terrorism and New Media
The post-Al Qaeda generation
Philip Seib and Dana M. Janbek

Global Terrorism and New Media

The post-Al Qaeda generation

Philip Seib and Dana M. Janbek

LONDON AND NEW YORK

First published 2011
by Routledge
2 Park Square, Milton Park, Abingdon, Oxon, OX14 4RN

Simultaneously published in the U.S.A. and Canada
by Routledge
270 Madison Ave, New York NY 10016

Routledge is an imprint of the Taylor & Francis Group, an informa business

Transferred to Digital Printing 2011

© 2011 Philip Seib and Dana M. Janbek

Typeset in Times New Roman by
Taylor & Francis Books

British Library Cataloguing in Publication Data
A catalogue record for this book is available from the British Library

Library of Congress Cataloging-in-Publication Data
Seib, Philip M., 1949-
Global terrorism and new media : the post Al-Qaeda generation / Philip
Seib and Dana M. Janbek.
   p. cm.
Includes bibliographical references and index.
1. Terrorism and mass media. 2. Terrorism–Computer network resources. 3.
Terrorists–Recruiting. 4. Internet–Political aspects. 5. Information warfare.
I. Janbek, Dana M. II. Title.
   P96.T47S45 2010
   363.325–dc22
                            2010006937

ISBN 978-0-415-77961-6 (hbk)
ISBN 978-0-415-77962-3 (pbk)
ISBN 978-0-203-84537-0 (ebk)

To the victims of the United States' 9/11 and Jordan's 9/11, and to others throughout the world whose lives have been affected by terrorism.

Contents

Preface

This book is not the first examination of terrorism and new media, nor will it be the last. That says as much about the durability of terrorism and its embrace of new media tools as it does about the persistence of those who write about such matters.

As a political force, terrorism has a long history and it has always evolved in order to survive and retain its ugly potency. During the first decade of the twenty-first century, terrorism has proved to be pervasive in terms of the incidence of terrorist acts, the pretensions to legitimacy of terrorists, the prominence of a few individual terrorist leaders, and, more significantly, in the way it has invaded our consciousness, permeating society with fearful awareness. The broad existence of a sense of terror, felt by some more acutely than by others, is a success for the purveyors of terrorism. There is no terrorism without communication, and this success has been enabled in part by clever use of new media, principally the numerous tools provided by the Internet.

The breadth of terrorism's societal presence is evidence that it is no longer the domain of the individual "mad bomber" or the isolated group of plotters intent on a single act or on a limited campaign designed primarily as a symbolic venture. Rather, today we see terrorism as an expansive enterprise, reliant on claims—however fraudulent—of religious or political legitimacy. Some terrorist organizations are conscious of building for the future, as can be seen in their insidious outreach to children. They nurture hatred and take advantage of ignorance and innocence to ensure that their ranks will fill faster than they can be depleted by counterterrorism measures.

This appeal to young people (as is discussed in Chapter 4) illustrates ways that new media have been woven into the fabric of terrorist enterprises. YouTube, as just one example, has proved an invaluable tool, allowing terrorist groups to advertise themselves in a venue that has innate attraction to a youthful audience. Without Internet-based media, terrorists would probably be unable to reach most of these prospective supporters. In terms of remaining visible to a larger, more general audience, the Internet similarly allows terrorist groups to thrive virtually, outside the shadows where they once had to dwell.

The relationship between terrorism and new media is important to several constituencies that address terrorism in different ways. For governments seeking to prevent terrorist attacks and to punish those who have carried out such attacks, new media add layers of complexity to terrorist organizations and operations. Whether the means of addressing terrorism is through military, law enforcement, or politics, the technologically sophisticated milieu in which many terrorists operate makes them both more elusive and more ubiquitous. This is the terrain on which they must be fought, as well as by using more traditional methods to find them and remove their operating capacity through capturing them or by enticing them to repudiate violence and rely instead on conventional political practices.

Members of the public must understand terrorism if they are to successfully deal with the terror produced by this enemy. Even if not directly or physically affected by terrorist attacks, people in many parts of the world must confront fear—of flying in an airplane, of traveling on a train or subway, of working in an office building, and even just driving down a street or going shopping. In the West, there is a tendency to focus on singular events such as the 9/11 attacks or the bombings in London and Madrid. But what about the Iraqis and Pakistanis and others who live every day with the very real possibility of a terrorist bombing? For people to exist without the emotional paralysis that terror can induce requires an understanding of the evil that is at work in their world. Broad-based comprehension of terrorism is also essential if the public is to have a voice in governmental responses. Before surrendering basic rights and values or acceding to bloody military action, people should understand who the enemy is, what motivates them, how they operate, and what is at stake.

To a large extent, these decisions made by the public are dependent on information they receive from the news media. Many journalists treat terrorism simplistically, focusing on individual terrorist acts and their immediate aftermath without thoughtfully inquiring why these acts occurred and exploring alternative ways to respond. The always-present tendency of the news media, even in democracies, to move in lockstep with government is particularly evident in matters related to terrorism. That will continue unless journalists become better schooled in the roots and practices of terrorism, and today that means appreciating the enhanced power terrorists enjoy as a result of their use of new media.

For the terrorists themselves, new media are, collectively, a transformative tool that offers endless possibilities for communication and expansion. The power of terrorism lies not in the acts of individuals but rather in the networks that allow secure coordination within even loosely knit terrorist organizations. New media are crucial in helping terrorist groups to endure—to sustain themselves by reaching various publics and to create a virtual impermeability that protects their operations. These media allow terrorist groups to become regional and even global players, sometimes punching above their weight in propaganda terms and building support from among those who might otherwise not even know of their existence. Dissemination of videos over the Internet, to cite just one example, enables terrorists to rely less on traditional news media to deliver their messages to widespread audiences.

With regard to security and operational matters, new media allow intelligent terrorists to work more effectively. As is discussed in this volume, to protect communications terrorist organizations have become adept at "cyber dead drops" and other tricks of their evolving trade. They can use publicly accessible tools, such as Google satellite mapping, e-mail, and text messages, to plan and execute their attacks.

Skillful use of media has also created misperceptions about how terrorism really works. Clever and persistent reliance on Internet-based media allowed Abu Musab al-Zarqawi, a murderous thug, to become a terrorist celebrity, eclipsing even Osama bin Laden during the height of Zarqawi's operations in Iraq. When he was killed by American bombs in 2006, his "stardom" led many news organizations and political figures to greatly overrate the positive results of his being removed from the conflict. Even the leaders of Al Qaeda, Osama bin Laden and Ayman al-Zawahiri, have seen their importance magnified to an inaccurate degree by their online presence.

In a celebrity culture, this is not surprising, but it can lead to dangerous misapprehensions about the realities of terrorism. Only part of the danger comes from the likes of bin Laden or Zarqawi. Those who actually wreak havoc are the young men who conducted attacks in London, Mumbai, and other cities, and the suicide bombers who have struck elsewhere so many times. The networks of which they are part rely not on the media exposure accorded to the "stars" but rather on the web of connections made possible by new media.

Treating terrorism realistically is one of the goals of this book. This is a difficult field in some ways, because much depends on the eye of the beholder. The notion that "one person's terrorist is another person's freedom fighter" holds up only occasionally. In truth, when terrorists are at work, innocents die. Ask the parents of Beslan, North Ossetia, if their children's deaths in their community's school was the work of freedom fighters or terrorists. The justifications offered for terrorist acts are flimsy at best, and most often are hideously amoral.

Nevertheless, examining terrorism means addressing a number of labeling issues. There is a difference between a terrorist who conducts murderous acts and an extremist who preaches radical change. There is also a difference between an insurgent who attacks the troops of an occupying army and the terrorist who indiscriminately kills civilians. Labeling an organization as "terrorist" is sometimes accurate, sometimes too sweeping. For instance, the U.S. State Department's list of foreign terrorist organizations included 45 groups as of January 2010. Among these is Hezbollah. Even if one assumes that some members of Hezbollah are terrorists, does that mean that everyone who belongs to Hezbollah is a terrorist? Certainly not. Hezbollah, Hamas, and some other organizations on the list play major political roles in their homelands, and their members include doctors, teachers, and others who have no intention of participating in or endorsing terrorism. So, labeling should be done with care.

Another issue encountered when studying terrorism is the use of the word "jihad." "Jihadi" and "terrorist" are often used interchangeably in the news media and elsewhere, but that approach is debatable. As noted by the religion scholar Karen Armstrong, the Arabic root of the word jihad "signifies a physical, moral, spiritual and intellectual effort." She wrote that numerous Arabic words denoted armed struggle, but jihad is truly "a struggle on all fronts—moral, spiritual, and political—to create a just and decent society." This internal jihad is distinguished from that related to war. Armstrong cited a hadith (traditional quotation) from the Prophet Mohammed on returning from battle: "We return from the little jihad to the greater jihad."[1]

An argument can be made that ceding jihad to terrorists allows them to claim moral high ground that they do not deserve. For both the "terrorist"/ "extremist" and "jihad" issues, we have tried to avoid using the terms in ways that are defined by the players themselves. We use "extremist" where we think it appropriate and limit references to "jihadi" and "jihadist." Nevertheless, particularly in the latter case, the usage of "jihadi" is so widespread that we retain it when authors to whom we are referring have themselves used it. This is not a satisfactory resolution of this issue, but we hope our readers will ponder this and consider the issues involved.

A more important matter concerns our concentration on terrorism that is perpetrated by Muslims. One of us grew up in an Arab Muslim society, and neither of us believes that Islam is a religion that supports hatred or terrorism. Certain realities, however, are inescapable. In 2004, after the Beslan school siege in which so many children died, the well-known Arab journalist Abdul Rahman al-Rashed wrote: "It is a certain fact that not all Muslims are terrorists, but it is equally certain, and exceptionally painful, that almost all terrorists are Muslims. What a pathetic record. What an abominable achievement. Does this tell us anything about ourselves, our societies, and our culture?"[2]

Such anguished introspection is not uncommon in the Muslim world, and we examine some of this. But for purposes of writing this book, we soon found that al-Rashed's comments referencing recent history were largely accurate, particularly within the context of our analysis. There are certainly non-Muslim terrorists operating around the world, but few of them use new media to the extent that Al Qaeda and its progeny do. We briefly discuss the activities of Colombia-based FARC and ELN, both of which have used new media (and, in FARC's case, been fought against through an Internet-based campaign). But when you plunge into the reservoir of material compiled by scholars, think tank experts, and other specialists in terrorism, you find a largely Muslim-centric discipline.

We discovered no way around this. To try to "balance" the contents of the book by including a comparable amount of material related to non-Muslim terrorist groups would be misleading.

The book's contents are as follows. Chapter 1, "Communicating Terror," addresses definitional matters related to terrorism. In Chapter 2, "High Tech Terror: Al Qaeda and Beyond," we analyze Al Qaeda per se and Al Qaeda as a model for terrorist activity as part of its own network and outside it. Chapter 3, "Terrorists' Online Strategies," examines specific ways that terrorist organizations work with the Internet to strengthen their organization, extend their reach, and mount their operations. In Chapters 4 and 5, "Targeting the Young" and "Women and Terrorism," we look at terrorist outreach (often extremely manipulative) to two vulnerable audiences. Chapter 6 explores "Terrorism's Online Future," and Chapter 7, "Responding to Terrorism" considers ways that the media tools used by terrorists can be turned against them.

We have sought to provide an overview supported by examples. Individual terrorist groups and specific terrorist acts may have their own substantial literature. We hope to have underscored one of the most challenging aspects related to terrorism's contemporary resiliency: the use of new media to expand terrorism's reach, enhance its organization, and convey the terror that sustains it. If this book encourages people to think more carefully about this, we will consider our efforts to have been worthwhile.

Acknowledgements

I would like to thank my colleagues at the University of Southern California, particularly the people I work with in the Center on Public Diplomacy, for their support as I have tried to balance my tasks as a scholar and an administrator. Working with Andrew Humphrys at Routledge has been a pleasure, and our literary agent Robbie Anna Hare deserves, as always, thanks for her dedication to our interests. Most importantly, I would like to thank the many people who work unceasingly to bring an end to the scourge of terrorism. These range from soldiers in firefights to scholars in libraries. I salute their efforts.

Philip Seib

I would like to sincerely thank my colleagues at Lasell College, and my former professors and colleagues at the University of Miami, for constantly encouraging me to pursue my research interests and inspiring me to do my best. Finally, I would like to encourage those who ask simple questions about terrorism to not settle for simple answers, and in their quest for knowledge, to always seek the multiple truths that could exist.

Dana M. Janbek

1 Communicating terror

Communication is at the heart of terrorism. The principal accomplishment of Al Qaeda on 9/11 was not killing several thousand people, but rather terrifying millions more through the reports and images of the attacks and changing the way many people throughout the world live. Furthermore, the global dissemination of news about that day's events advanced Al Qaeda's political agenda, giving credence to the organization's claims that it is the champion of Muslims long victimized by the infidel West and apostate Arab governments.

This chapter addresses terrorism as a communicative act and explains how tightly woven are terrorists' violent acts and their communication strategies. The most visible (which perhaps means most successful) terrorist groups are those that operate with a communication model that has advanced beyond simple delivery of a message to a passive audience. Rather, the modern communication model used by terrorist organizations is audience-based, meaning-centered, culture-dependent, and always tied into an ongoing narrative stream that is part of the socio-political context in which these organizations operate.[1]

As for terrorism itself, some fundamental points must be examined:

- how "terrorism" is defined;
- who is a "terrorist" and not a "freedom fighter";
- what is the magnitude of the threat posed by terrorists' use of the Internet and other media tools, including manipulation of conventional news coverage.

The media collectively constitute terrorism's oxygen, and how media-spread fear and anger affect the public is something terrorists understand well.

Searching for definitions

The U.S. National Counterterrorism Center (NCTC) reported approximately 11,800 terrorist attacks against noncombatants in 2008, resulting in 54,000 deaths, injuries, or kidnappings. Of the 235 "high-casualty attacks" in which 10 or more people were killed, 75 percent occurred in the Near East or South Asia. More than 50 percent of those killed were Muslims, mostly in Iraq, Pakistan, and Afghanistan.[2]

Beyond such broad statistical summaries, details about specific attacks are not always available. The NCTC relies on open source information, and its report notes that "the perpetrators of over 7,000 attacks, or over 60 percent, in 2008 could not be determined." Terrorist groups splinter, false claims are made, and allegations are denied, making verifiable reporting difficult. A haze of imprecision hovers over terrorism analysis, complicating the task of those who want to study and understand terrorism, and perhaps respond to it.

The NCTC addresses some of the difficulties encountered when creating its statistical reports about terrorism. According to the Center, a "terrorist attack" occurred when

> subnational or clandestine groups or individuals deliberately or recklessly attacked civilians or noncombatants (including military personnel and assets outside war zones and war-like settings). Determination of what constitutes a terrorist act, however, can be more art than science; information is often incomplete, fact patterns may be open to interpretation, and perpetrators' intent is rarely clear.[3]

Similarly, "terrorism" has yet to be defined in a way that satisfies law enforcement, military, political, and public constituencies. U.S. law defines terrorism as "premeditated, politically motivated violence perpetrated against noncombatant targets by sub-national groups or clandestine agents, usually intended to influence an audience."[4] That is nicely lawyerly, but when parsed it leads to questions. What, exactly, is "politically" motivated? How narrowly are "noncombatant targets" defined? What are "sub-national" groups, particularly vis-à-vis transnational or other groups whose allegiances rest outside any relationship to nations, and what happens to "state terrorism" within this definition? What constitutes the intent to "influence an audience"?

Answers to these and related questions can be found, but they tend to lack consistency. Further complicating the search for a definition are variations even within a government's bureaucracy. In the United States, rather than accepting just the statutory definition, the Department of Defense has its own version: "The calculated use of unlawful violence or threat of unlawful violence to inculcate fear; intended to coerce or intimidate governments or societies in the pursuit of goals that are generally political, religious, or ideological."[5]

One facet of the definitional problem emerges in considering the aphorism, "One person's terrorist is another person's freedom fighter." Yasser Arafat? Menachem Begin? Others who rose through the ranks of bloody insurgencies to become prominent leaders? Should they be regarded as terrorists or freedom fighters? Is targeting of civilians during a conventional war, as in the firestorms of Dresden and Tokyo near the end of World War II, an act of terrorism, or is this a legitimate way to try to force an enemy government to surrender? Does perception take precedence over legalistic definition: were the Americans during the Revolutionary War honorable patriots or terroristic rebels? Americans and Britons might have decidedly different views about this. Would it matter if the Americans' primary targets had been civilian colonists loyal to England rather than the English troops?

A further dimension of this issue is the distinction between "terrorist" and "extremist." The latter might be a group that preaches hatred and in a non-specific way urges the targeting of noncombatants but does not directly engage in the prescribed actions. Also, their messages might remain outside the definition of terrorism by, for instance, calling for attacks on combatants but not civilians. Is a group endorsing, but not conducting, attacks on U.S. troops in Afghanistan a "terrorist" organization or something else? What about Hamas or Hezbollah, which are considered to be terrorist groups by some, but are regarded by many Palestinians and Lebanese (and others elsewhere in the world) as legitimate political organizations that claim the noble purpose of defending their homelands against occupiers?

There is also a proclivity, especially in the West, for applying "terrorist" to members of "the other" as defined by ethnicity, religion, or other criteria, but to be slower in doing so to homegrown terrorists. In the United States, "Osama bin Laden" and "terrorist" are synonymous, but that is not the case with Timothy McVeigh, the Caucasian U.S. Army veteran who bombed the Federal Building in Oklahoma City in April 1995, killing 168 people. In Great Britain in the aftermath of the 7/7 bombings of 2005, the perpetrators' identification as Muslims took precedence over recognition that three of the four had been born in Britain (and the fourth had been born in Jamaica).

Another definitional problem involves the use of the words "jihad" and "jihadi." Popular usage, by the news media and many commentators, equates jihad with terrorism or "holy war," and "jihadi" is freely used in referring to terrorists. Further, "radicalization" and "jihadization" are often used interchangeably, as can be seen in a report by the United States Senate Committee on Homeland Security and Governmental Affairs, which cited the e-book, *39 Ways To Serve and Participate in Jihad*, as evidence of this. This e-book is easily found, in English, on the Web. According to the Senate report, it tells its readers that "a supporter of violent Islamist ideology can aid the movement in myriad ways, including joining the movement in spirit, fundraising, or pursuing … 'electronic jihad,'" which is defined as participating in online chat rooms, disseminating propaganda, and aiding cyberattacks against enemy Web sites.[6]

But to treat jihad in such a one-sided way is a simplistic approach, and there are alternative ways to define it. Karen Armstrong has written that jihad "remains a duty for Muslims to commit themselves to a struggle on all fronts—moral, spiritual, and political—to create a just and decent society, where the poor and vulnerable are not exploited, in the way that God had intended man to live."[7] (Based on this view of jihad, "Jihad" is used in Arabic as a male name.) That is much more benign usage than is common today in counterterrorism and antiterrorism circles, and among terrorists themselves. It can be argued that extremists have hijacked a fine concept and altered it to serve their own purposes.

In this debate about "jihad," the Combating Terrorism Center at the U.S. Military Academy has grappled with definitional issues and has come down on the side of using jihad as a synonym for Muslim terrorism. The Center offers this explanation:

> We recognize that the use of "Jihadi" to designate Salafis of a militant stripe is controversial. Some analysts feel that it cedes too much to militant Salafis to ratify their use of the term—they call their movement *al-haraka al-jihadiyya* ("the Jihadi Movement")—since jihad has positive connotations in Islam. However, we have opted to use it for the following reasons. First, it has wide currency in the Western counterterrorism community. Second, the proposed alternatives are either too imprecise or polemically charged to be analytically useful. Third, "Jihadism" indicates the centrality of religious warfare in the militant Salafi worldview. Fourth, using the label makes Jihadis accountable for giving the term a bad name and for not living up to the high standard of conduct associated with jihad. Finally, the term is used in Arab media and was coined by a devout Saudi Muslim who is hostile to the ideology, so it is not a Western neologism.[8]

In terms of raising questions about moral justification for "terror" and the identity of "terrorists," such matters provide fine fuel for debate, but for those who enforce the law, report the news, and simply try to understand the world, debate needs to eventually give way to a broadly acceptable definition.

Bruce Hoffman, one of the leading terrorism scholars, has done a better job than most. He defines terrorism as

> the deliberate creation and exploitation of fear through violence or the threat of violence in the pursuit of political change. ... Terrorism is specifically designed to have far-reaching psychological effects beyond the immediate victim(s) or object of the terrorist attack. ... Through the publicity generated by their violence, terrorists seek to obtain the leverage, influence, and power they otherwise lack to effect political change on either a local or an international scale.[9]

Hoffman's emphasis on the creation and exploitation of fear, and using that fear to obtain political leverage is particularly significant because it underscores the point that terrorism is a *political* crime; it is not thrill-killing (although it may become that for some of its operatives), but rather is seen as a strategic tool and an equalizer in asymmetric conflict. How does an aggrieved political entity take on a powerful state that is deemed an enemy? Without justifying the strategy of Al Qaeda, how else, other than terrorism, could it challenge the United States in a way that would establish itself as a viable opponent of a superpower and attract the attention of publics that it considers its constituency? Conventional warfare is clearly not an option for an organization such as Al Qaeda that declares war against the United States, as Osama bin Laden did in 1996. In that statement, bin Laden cited the continuing presence of U.S. troops in Saudi Arabia and said, "Terrorizing you, while you are carrying arms in our land, is a legitimate right and a moral obligation."[10]

Writing before the current fascination with terrorism developed, Michael Walzer noted that "the systematic terrorizing of whole populations" has been used by "established governments as well as radical movements." In World War II, both the Allied and the Axis powers targeted civilian populations, or at least showed little regard for their safety. The purpose of terrorism, wrote Walzer, "is to destroy the morale of a nation or a class, to undercut its solidarity; its method is the random murder of innocent people." Randomness, he adds, is an essential part of this. Death must come by chance and with enough frequency that civilians "feel themselves fatally exposed and demand that their governments negotiate for their safety."[11]

Of course, this often doesn't work as planned. Hitler's attempt to terrorize the British people into demanding negotiations with Germany instead intensified their resolve to fight. Americans may have been "terrorized" by the September 11, 2001 attacks, but most then wanted their government to retaliate, certainly not negotiate.

The obvious likelihood of such responses by publics and governments illustrates the futility of terrorism in most instances and its intrinsic criminality. Looking at terrorism with detached objectivity, it is easy to conclude that only the exceptionally stupid or deranged would believe that their acts of terror would achieve the substantive political change that presumably was the goal of the terrorist action. Al Qaeda's adherents might argue that the 9/11 attacks led to the United States engaging in a self-destructive war in Iraq, but the attacks were really an excuse, not a cause, for that war. Theoretically, persistent terrorist attacks might wear down a country's willingness to cling to policies that terrorists use to justify the attacks, but—so far, at least—terrorist organizations have not possessed the breadth of operational capacity necessary for such staying power. Even years of attacks in Northern Ireland and Palestine/Israel did not bring about the substantive change that the attacks' perpetrators wanted.

Terrorism in the form of suicide bombing attacks directed against civilians may illustrate the link between terror and politics. In 1996, Hamas conducted a series of terror bombings that killed more than 60 Israeli civilians within several days. The result was not Israel backing down, but, more predictably, a backlash that helped to elect Binyamin Netanyahu, whose obstructionist approach to dealing with Palestinians enhanced the relatively extremist position of Hamas within the Palestinians' contentious political camps. Yasser Arafat's Palestinian Authority asked religious leaders to condemn the attacks on the grounds that Islam forbids suicide, while Hamas asked other religious authorities to pronounce the attacks to be a legitimate form of jihad.[12]

This case (which is not unique) illustrates that the politics of terror may involve motivations related to internal politics; in this instance, not just Palestinians versus Israelis, but also Palestinians versus Palestinians.

Looking at the variety of actions that constitute terrorism, it is clear that in many instances, acts of terrorism are symbolic murders that their perpetrators attempt to legitimize by identifying them as political acts. Defining terrorism will continue to be an exercise for politicians, law enforcement officials, academics, and others, including those who incite and commit the acts. Arriving at a definition is most important when an alleged terrorist faces judicial process, but beyond that, determining why and how terrorists act as they do has greater practical value.

The terrorist's identity[13]

Profiles of known terrorists have disposed of the notion that terrorism's ranks are filled with ignorant young people acting out of mindless rage. Instead, terrorists often emerge from the middle class or higher, they are well-educated, and they understand the likely effects of their actions on others and themselves. They act out of frustration, anger about perceived injustices, and a sense of disenfranchisement. These motivations are often bolstered by self-justification grounded in religious, ethnic, or nationalistic factors. Politically based reluctance to acknowledge the breadth of terrorism's roots further deters the search for greater definitional precision.

It is unacceptably facile to excuse terrorism by arguing "they had no other way." That amounts to abandonment of hope for a civil society and accepts the inevitability of violence in a world of imperfect governance. Similarly, however, it is unrealistic to dismiss the root causes of political discontent that may nurture terrorism as well as legitimate political action. Determining definitions related to "terrorism" is judgmental, but that is appropriate because the essence of morality is judgment. This is a task individuals and institutions must undertake.

Among those institutions are news organizations, which have significant effect on public perceptions of what is acceptable and unacceptable conduct in politics, conflict, and related matters. If the news media adopt simplistic formulations about terrorism, they will mislead the public.

The notion of an "independent press" is in itself simplistic. Every news organization requires financial support from private or public sources, and so the interests of those sources cannot be ignored. Further, even in countries where government cannot wield formal control over the news media, shrewd political leaders know how to manipulate news coverage. News executives, like politicians, read opinion surveys and often move with the public rather than try to take it in new directions.

This conformist tendency has been apparent in the aftermath of terrorist attacks, such as those in the United States in 2001. Most of the American media reacted reflexively, demanding revenge as justice rather than raising questions about why the attacks had happened and questioning how U.S. policy may have been a factor. Rare were voices such as that of Susan Sontag, who wrote in the *New Yorker* immediately after the attacks that those "licensed to follow the event seem to have joined together in a campaign to infantilize the public. Where is the acknowledgement that this was not a 'cowardly' attack on 'civilization' or 'liberty' or 'humanity' or 'the free world,' but an attack on the world's self-proclaimed superpower, undertaken as a consequence of specific American alliances and actions?"[14]

Sontag's point is not particularly profound, but it is notable for being so unusual in post-9/11 America. It was very much out of step with most media coverage in the United States and much of the rest of the world. She underscored the fact that a terrorist act is not merely about perpetrators and victims in isolation, but rather involves complex geopolitical issues that provide the context for such attacks.

Despite the importance of this larger political context, images—the simpler the better—often drive short-term responses to terrorism. Bethami Dobkin observed that television news, in particular, "complements a political process that is reliant on public images for legitimacy and guidance."[15] In the case of the 9/11 attacks, images of the World Trade Center were so vivid and disconcerting that they dominated public perception of the event and overwhelmed any instinct to ask why this had happened. There was little pushback from the news media, which seemed intent on enhancing the emotionalism of the moment rather than doing real journalism in which skepticism is not drowned by waves of "patriotism."

Such journalistic lapses can create a de facto symbiotic relationship between terrorists and news media. Sensational violence guarantees heavy news coverage, and, as Joseph Tuman has observed, "the desire for maximum publicity creates a tendency in terrorist violence to select targets and engage in types of symbolic action translate well visually in coverage and broadcast." Tuman went on to say:

> Though terrorists may feel they are manipulating media in selecting targets for this purpose and engaging in sensational violence to ensure coverage, the opposite is actually true. In a world with media saturation, and news stories already devoted to coverage of so many issues relating to violence, death, and tragedy, guaranteeing coverage of a terrorism story requires visually compelling, dramatic, and therefore devastating violence on a larger and larger scale; sadly, this also means that with each act of terror the threshold for what is dramatic and truly terrifying must be raised.[16]

Therefore, the news media play a central role in defining what "terrorism" is and what is merely "criminal." Terrorist organizations such as Al Qaeda are fully aware of how this process works and plan their actions accordingly. Brigitte Nacos has noted that "most terrorists calculate the consequences of their deeds, the likelihood of gaining media attention, and, most important, the likelihood of winning entrance—through the media—to the "triangle of political communication,"[17] which consists of the mass media, the public, and the government. In other words, the terrorists can use the media as a way to inject themselves into the conversation of civil society.

In the aftermath of the 9/11 attacks, the international news organizations that recognized that not everyone in the world sympathized with the super-power victim quickly found that politics would shape even the semantics of coverage. Shortly after the 9/11 attacks, Reuters news service began using "hijackers" rather than "terrorists" to describe the perpetrators, a decision that was angrily criticized by those who saw Reuters as catering to anti-American sentiment. Citing Reuters's "longstanding policy against the use of emotive terms," Stephen Jukes, head of global news for Reuters, said in an internal memo, "We do not characterize the subjects of news stories but instead report their actions, identity, or backgrounds," thereby letting news consumers "make their own decisions based on the facts."[18]

How those facts are framed, however, affects that decision-making. Despite often conscientious efforts on the parts of individual journalists and their news organizations to remain "neutral" (in terrorism-related stories as in other cases), wielding influence is unavoidable. Similarly, being influenced to varying degrees is also unavoidable. Terrorists can force coverage of their actions by making them particularly dramatic, but government can also influence the tone and substance of terrorism coverage, including the terminology used in such coverage.[19]

Some news organizations have grappled with these matters, thinking about the meaning and effect of words and trying to maintain consistency in the use of words. In its style guide, the British newspaper, the *Guardian*, addressed the terrorism/terrorist issue this way:

> Whatever one's political sympathies, suicide bombers, the 9/11 attackers and most paramilitary groups can all reasonably be regarded as terrorists (or at least groups some of whose members perpetrate terrorist acts). ... Often, alternatives such as militants, radicals, separatists, etc., may be more appropriate and less controversial, but this is a difficult area: references to the "resistance," for example, imply more sympathy to a cause than calling such fighters "insurgents." The most important thing is that, in news reporting, we are not seen—because of the language we use—to be taking sides.[20]

The *New York Times* does not have a formal policy regarding use of "terrorism" and "terrorist," but the newspaper's public editor, Clark Hoyt, addressed the issue after the attacks in Mumbai in late 2008. The *Times* coverage referred to the men who carried out the attacks as "militants," "gunmen," "attackers," and "assailants," but not "terrorists." The Mumbai attacks, wrote Hoyt,

> posed a familiar semantic issue for *Times* editors: what to call people who pursue political, religious, territorial, or unidentifiable goals through violence on civilians. Many readers want the newspaper, even on the news pages, to share their moral outrage—or their political views—by adopting

the word terrorist, with all its connotations of opprobrium. What you call someone matters. If he is a terrorist, he is an enemy of all civilized people, and his cause is less worthy of consideration. In the newsroom and at overseas bureaus, especially Jerusalem, there has been a lot of soul-searching about the terminology of terrorism. Editors and reporters have asked whether, to avoid the appearance of taking sides, the paper bends itself into a pretzel or risks appearing callous to abhorrent acts. They have wrestled with questions like why those responsible for the 9/11 attacks are called terrorists but the murderers of a little girl in her bed in a Jewish settlement are not. And whether, if the use of the word terrorist can be interpreted as a political act, not using it is one too.

Hoyt noted that the newspaper's former Jerusalem bureau chief, James Bennet, had written a memo about exercising restraint when using terror-related terms. Bennet wrote that he initially avoided the word terrorism altogether and thought it more useful to describe an attack in as vivid detail as possible so readers could decide their own labels. But he came to believe that never using the word "felt so morally neutral as to be a little sickening. The calculated bombing of students in a university cafeteria, or of families gathered in an ice-cream parlor, cries out to be called what it is," he wrote.

Underscoring the differences of opinion within the newspaper, Hoyt wrote:

> I do not think it is possible to write a set of hard and fast rules for the T-words, and I think *The Times* is both thoughtful about them and maybe a bit more conservative in their use than I would be.
>
> My own broad guideline: If it looks as if it was intended to sow terror and it shocks the conscience, whether it is planes flying into the World Trade Center, gunmen shooting up Mumbai, or a political killer in a little girl's bedroom, I'd call it terrorism—by terrorists.[21]

The *Washington Post* developed guidelines that said in part:

> Terrorism and terrorist can be useful words, but they are labels. Like all labels, they do not convey much hard information. ... When we use these labels we should do so in ways that are not tendentious. For example, we should not resolve the argument over whether Hamas is a terrorist organization, or a political organization that condones violence, or something else, by slapping a label on Hamas. Instead we should give readers facts and perhaps quotes from disputing parties about how best to characterize the organization.[22]

Words matter. Referring to someone as a "terrorist" or "murderer" rather than using "resistance fighter" or "martyr" can, over time, make a significant difference in how the public perceives particular persons and actions. Related to this is the need to avoid lapsing into stereotyping. In the United States and

Western Europe plenty of evidence exists about the existence of anti-Arab and anti-Muslim sentiment. The news media (and the entertainment media) can do much to either encourage or discourage simplistic public attitudes that are often just a short step away from hatred and its consequences.

Semantics can be shaped by politics, and the news media must be counted on to make thoughtful choices among descriptive terms, just as they must describe events without spin or other bias. Popular usage often follows the lead of the mass media, and so the environment in which terroristic actions are judged will be shaped to a considerable extent by the contest among words.

Terrorism as communication

In his evaluation of Al Qaeda and other terrorist organizations, sociology and communications scholar Manuel Castells observed that such groups rely on two main tactics of action: terror and media politics. Of the latter, he wrote:

> Ultimately, the action is geared toward human minds, toward transform-
> ing consciousness. The media, local and global, are the means of com-
> munication through which the public mind is formed. Therefore, action
> has to be media oriented, it has to be spectacular, provide good footage,
> so that the whole world can see it: like a Hollywood movie because this is
> what has trained the human mind in our times.[23]

Merely killing people or blowing up things does not accomplish terrorists' purpose. A simple model for terror effects uses concentric circles. At the core is the damage—deaths and physical destruction—caused by the terroristic act itself. This is certainly significant; it would be improper to minimize the importance of loss of life and, to a lesser extent, loss of property. But unless weap-
ons of mass destruction are employed, the damage will be contained and its impact will similarly be limited to those who lose their lives and property and those with immediate interest, such as family members and property owners. Unless the terrorists had sought to kill particular individuals or destroy a particular physical asset, their success in terrorizing through the act per se will be narrow.

Their success expands exponentially as reports and images of the act reach larger publics. The next circle comprises local media from the affected area that are seen by audiences familiar with the site, and perhaps with the victims, of the attack. Personal attachments are likely to lead to more visceral reactions.

Beyond that circle are more distant news consumers. Those without physi-
cal or political connection to the attack may be only moderately moved by the news, but no matter how distant, some are likely to shudder with a sense of terror. How many people get onto an airplane, even today, without some kind of 9/11-memory-based flinch? How many regular train riders, wherever they might reside, were unaffected by the 2004 bombings in Madrid that killed almost 200 persons and injured almost 2,000 more? On the other hand,

people with no connections to train-riding or to Spain may have felt a less personal connection and have been less moved except for a general feeling of sadness about the loss of life, or anger about the savagery of the act.

All but the centermost of these rings are linked to the event by mass media, primarily widely accessible news media, but also self-generated media that terrorist organizations use with increasing skill. Most mainstream news organizations impose standards that rule out graphic images from terror attacks, but the perpetrators of such attacks might disseminate those images through the Internet and other new media sources to audiences that are smaller but are considered high-value, such as potential recruits. The terrorist groups also know that videos on YouTube or other online venues can reach substantial audiences regardless of how much attention is paid to these items by traditional media outlets. Videos showing the execution by terrorists of kidnap victims have sometimes been viewed online millions of times. Overall, getting words and images to various publics is far easier in this era of fewer determinative information gatekeepers.

Even within the ranks of conventional media organizations, certain editorial predispositions lend themselves to exploitation, or at least to simplistic formulations that poorly serve the public. Treatment of the idea of a "clash of civilizations" is one facet of the news media's approach to coverage of terrorism.[24]

The "call to jihad is rising in the streets of Europe, and is being answered," reported the *New York Times* in April 2004. The *Times* story quoted a Muslim cleric in Britain who had been touting the "culture of martyrdom," an imam in Switzerland urging his followers to "impose the will of Islam on the godless society of the West," and another radical Islamist leader in Britain predicting that "our Muslim brothers from abroad will come one day and conquer here, and then we will live under Islam in dignity."[25]

For those who believe that a clash of civilizations—particularly between Islam and the non-Islamic West—is under way or at least approaching, the provocative comments in the *Times* article were evidence that "the clash" is not merely a figment of an overheated political imagination. Ever since Samuel Huntington presented his theory about such a clash in a *Foreign Affairs* article in 1993, debate has continued about whether his ideas are substantive or off the mark. (It should be noted that the term "clash of civilizations" was coined by another scholar, Bernard Lewis, in 1990.[26]) For the news media, this debate is important because it helps shape their approach to covering the world. For terrorists, the conversation about the purported clash is also significant because it provides a rationale for their actions—a "them-against-us" framing of their violence.

In Huntington's article, which he refined and expanded in his 1996 book, *The Clash of Civilizations and the Remaking of World Order*, he argued that "the clash of civilizations will dominate global politics. The fault lines between civilizations will be the battle lines of the future."[27] In the book, Huntington said that "culture and cultural identities, which at the broadest level are civilization identities, are shaping the patterns of cohesion, disintegration, and conflict in the post-Cold War world." Huntington's corollaries to this proposition, in summary form, are these:

- "For the first time in history, global politics is both multipolar and multi-civilizational."
- As the balance of power among civilizations shifts, the relative influence of the West is declining.
- A world order is emerging that is civilization-based.
- "Universalist pretensions" are increasingly bringing the West into conflict with other civilizations, especially the Islamic world and China.
- If the West is to survive, America must reaffirm its Western identity and unite with other Westerners in the face of challenges from other civilizations.[28]

One reason that Huntington's clash theory initially had appeal was that policymakers, the news media, and others were moving uncertainly into the post-Cold War era without much sense of how the newest world order was taking shape. They were receptive to a new geopolitical scheme, particularly one that featured identifiable adversarial relationships that would supersede those being left behind. The confrontational alignment of nations and ideologies during the Cold War's half-century had been convenient for the news media as well as for policymakers. The American perspective was that the bad guys operated from Moscow and its various outposts, while the good guys were based in Washington and allied countries. Not all the world accepted such a facile division, but those who did found it tidy and easy to understand. Many American news organizations shaped their coverage to conform to this worldview; there was Cold War journalism just as there was Cold War politics.

But when the Cold War more or less ended and its principal threat—nuclear conflict between the two superpowers—was no longer a concern, interest in international news became less acute. New villains could be found from time to time—Saddam Hussein was one who filled the bill nicely—but they were not part of a grand scenario such as that of the Cold War. Even the 1991 Gulf War seemed to take place in a narrow context. In response to an act of aggression that the American government judged to be against its interests, the United States built a coalition and smashed the aggressor. It was a fine showcase for America in its unipolar moment, but it seemed little more than a response to a singular aberrant act. At that time, Saddam Hussein's Iraq was not seen by most in the region or elsewhere as representing any larger cultural or political force, and certainly not a threat to global order (except in the sense of endangering the flow of oil, for which he was promptly spanked).

Nevertheless, something was percolating. In 1993, a car bomb killed seven and injured hundreds at the World Trade Center in New York. In 1995, an alleged plot to blow up a dozen U.S. aircraft was foiled. In 1995 and 1996, truck bombs were used in attacks on American training facilities and residences in Saudi

Arabia. In 1998, U.S. embassies in Kenya and Tanzania were attacked with car bombs. In 2000, the USS *Cole* was attacked by suicide bombers in Yemen.

These and other terrorist incidents received substantial news coverage, but primarily as isolated events. Neither the government nor the news media connected the dots or tried to make sense of what was happening as part of political change in the world. Although the 9/11 attacks on the United States represented a staggering escalation, they were part of this continuum of terrorism, and as such should have evoked less surprise. The attacks on American targets throughout the 1990s, as well as incidents directed at non-American targets (such as a 1995 assassination attempt against Egyptian president Hosni Mubarak), were parts of a radical Islamist agenda designed by Osama bin Laden and others who staged these attacks as a way to eventually force governments to respond to Al Qaeda's demands related to alleged oppression of Muslims and Islam's status in the world.

Bin Laden himself was a shadowy presence, but not invisible. He was known to numerous governments, had been indicted for the 1998 embassy bombings, and granted interviews to Western news organizations. He told CNN in 1997, "We declared jihad against the U.S. government," and said to ABC in 1998, "We anticipate a black future for America."[29]

Bin Laden does not in himself constitute a "civilization" that is clashing with the West. He can be dismissed as a murderer who has merely proclaimed himself to be a defender of Islam. There is, however, more to a decade of terrorism than one man's persistence. Bin Laden has tapped into widespread resentment about how those with power treat those without it, and particularly how Muslims remain oppressed by their own governments and much of the non-Islamic world. (This state of affairs is implicitly contrasted with the "golden age" of Islam centuries earlier, when the Muslim world's contributions to civilization were unmatched by those of other cultures.) Even while he has, presumably, been cornered somewhere near the Afghanistan-Pakistan border, others have embraced his cause.

Whether Huntington's theory is validated by terrorist events directed by bin Laden and others, and whether Huntington's view of civilizational conflict should guide the planning of news coverage remains debatable. In news coverage, as in politics, a vacuum exists if there is no "enemy." Adeed Dawisha wrote that "in the wake of the demise of international communism, the West saw radical Islam as perhaps its most dangerous adversary."[30] Thus, an enemy; and so a vacuum no more. Islam's usefulness in this regard was apparent immediately after the 2001 attacks, when mainstream American newspapers featured headlines such as these: "This Is a Religious War"; "Yes, This Is About Islam"; "Muslim Rage"; "The Deep Intellectual Roots of Islamic Terror"; "Kipling Knew What the US May Now Learn"; "Jihad 101"; and so on. Several new stories discussed the Crusades and were illustrated with pictures of Richard the Lionheart.[31]

Events have pushed many in the news media toward a de facto adoption of the Huntington theory, regardless of its many critics, because it seems to provide a convenient framework for making sense of new kinds of conflict. The public in numerous Western nations has followed this lead. In the United States, with its minimal Muslim population, Islam is off-handedly relegated to the status of a dangerously exotic "other." In some European countries, however, the growing number of Muslims is more controversial.

The 9/11 attacks, the resulting Afghanistan War, and the Iraq War begun in 2003 lend themselves to political and journalistic shorthand: We have a new array of villains, and they have Islam in common (although their countries' religious diversity is overlooked). And so, some believe, this means that a clash of civilizations is under way. The continuing debate about the clash theory gives news organizations, particularly in the United States, an opportunity to reassess post-Cold War—and now post-9/11—alignments of political and cultural forces throughout the world. In doing so, the news media, like policymakers and the public, should guard against accepting convenient stereotypes and judging civilizational differences in simplistic ways. When Huntington's first clash article appeared in 1993, it seemed to support inchoate fears and reinforce Western predispositions about "the others," and it offered a new version of the Cold War's "us and them" dichotomy. But just because the public may be prepared to accept an idea does not mean that news organizations should treat it uncritically. Journalists have a responsibility to explain, to contribute to an intellectual debate that news consumers may use to build their understanding of issues. Failure to do so—lapsing into stereotyping and other simplistic techniques—fosters dangerous know-nothingism.

The embrace by some media organizations of Huntington's ideas has made it seem that the threat of "civilizational clash" is acceptable as conventional wisdom. This has elicited responses from Islamic leaders, such as Mustafa Ceric, the Grand Mufti of Bosnia, who observed that Islam should not be labeled a "terrorist religion," because "the violent small minority of any faith does not represent the peaceful great majority of that faith."[32]

Ceric's point is valid; there are approximately 1.3 billion Muslims in the world and obviously only a small number of them belong to Al Qaeda and like-minded organizations that engage in terrorist activities. There are, however, those who for their own purposes step away from such logic as Ceric offers because they wish to foster a violent clash of civilizations. A case can be made that this is a goal of Al Qaeda, and if so, the chances of reaching that goal are enhanced by the opinion among many Muslims that the purpose of the American invasion of Iraq was in part "to weaken the Muslim world."[33]

The news media today confront an international community that is more amorphous than in the past. Today's "enemies" (as defined by Western governments and media), such as Al Qaeda, often have no home that can be identified on a map and no collective space that can be targeted by the military and demonized by the public. There is no Nazi Germany or Soviet Union in an era when "virtual states" can define their existence by relying on technology rather than conventional borders. That produces disorientation among policymakers, journalists, and news consumers alike. It is hard to plan policy or design news coverage without being able to rely on traditional tools such as maps and governments around the world.

These issues extend beyond the civilizational conflicts that Huntington described. Policymakers and journalists have similar interests in grappling with these matters. The 9/11 Commission's report addressed the need to engage in a "struggle of ideas."[34] News coverage is part of that. While governments decide how to adapt to these new realities, the news business must realign its own priorities if journalists are to help the public develop a better sense of what is going on in the world. Samuel Huntington's definitions may be questioned and his conclusions challenged, but he performed a considerable service by pushing policymakers and journalists toward undertaking a more sophisticated analysis of how the world works. That analysis is by no means completed, and until it is part of the foundation of terrorism will remain only partly understood.

Islam's media identity

An alternative to Huntington's view is to see a clash *within* Islam between moderates and reactionaries as the truly crucial struggle. This contest also relies on communication to promote different ideological stances and different strategies. Because mass communication provides the most commonly used political forums, each side tries to use media most convincingly and attract the most adherents. As with media-savvy political competitors elsewhere, importance is attached not just to the content of the message, but how it is presented. This extends into religious messages; like Christianity's "TV preachers," Islam has "TV imams," old school and new school.

Among the old school religious leaders is Yusuf al-Qaradawi, who, through his presence on Al Jazeera and Islam Online, established himself as one of the Islamic world's best-known public figures.[35] Born in 1926, al-Qaradawi studied theology at al-Azhar University and spent time in an Egyptian prison because of his ties to the Muslim Brotherhood. He has written about the Islamic awakening—his many books have sold in the hundreds of thousands—and emphasized the important role of the *ulama* (religious scholars) as its leaders. He has championed the independence of the *ulama* and argued that Islam requires freedom of thought and discussion.[36]

Al-Qaradawi has proved adept at shaping his message to meet the demands of new media. As Jon Anderson noted, he is "wholly orthodox in theology but expressing it in a more modern idiom that attracts a transnational audience among professional middle classes."[37] Modern does not mean moderate. Al-Qaradawi has endorsed suicide bombing attacks on Israeli civilians as a legitimate tactic in the effort to reclaim Muslim territory.[38] He also, however, issued a *fatwa* that defends democracy not as a form of unbelief but as a system that properly gives people the right to choose their leaders without compulsion and to question and remove them. On another occasion, he denounced Abu Musab al-Zarqawi, leader of Al Qaeda in Iraq, as a murderer.[39]

Whatever al-Qaradawi's views on particular issues may be, he unquestionably wields greater influence by virtue of being a media personality. His political clout as "the global mufti" is enhanced by the reach and frequency that satellite television and the Internet provide. Al-Qaradawi and numerous other public figures constitute an expanding religious-political group that makes sophisticated use of new media. Gary Bunt observed that

> for an elite, the Internet now forms part of a religious conceptual framework, incorporating symbols, divine utterances, sacred texts, and the power to inspire and motivate individuals in both their personal practice and in wider worldly and sacred goals. ... It is through a digital interface that an increasing number of people will view their religion and their place in the Muslim world.[40]

A newer generation of media religious leaders is exemplified by Amr Khaled (born in 1967).[41] Alterman wrote,

> Through huge revival-style events in Egypt and increasingly via satellite television broadcasts beamed throughout the Middle East, Khaled has created not just a community of viewers, but also a community of participants. His followers do more than write and call in to his programs. His increasingly global audience participates in charity drives, organizes study groups, and seeks to apply his specific lessons to their daily lives.[42]

Favoring European suits and polo shirts rather than a cleric's robes, Khaled relies on Western vernacular, as when he talks about Islam "empowering" women and describes the Prophet Mohammed as "the first manager." Born in Egypt and now living in England, Khaled has built a huge following by explaining how Islam can thrive in the modern world. Second-generation European Muslims constitute a considerable part of his audience. His programs on Iqraa, a Saudi-owned satellite channel, reach millions of devoted viewers. His Web site, which received 26 million hits in 2005, is the third most popular Arabic site (behind Al Jazeera and an e-mail portal) and is translated into 16 other languages.

He tells women that they must wear the *hijab*, but—unlike al-Qaradawi—he does not often offer opinions on matters such as whether people should join the Palestinian or Iraqi resistance. His principal themes include fostering an Arab and Islamic revival by increasing literacy and community involvement. When addressing European Muslims, he stresses the importance of coexistence—for those living in the U.K., rooting for a British soccer team, not Pakistan's; and for those in France, lobbying for the legal right to wear the *hijab* in school, but in the meantime making do with designer hats.[43]

Khaled's example illustrates the multidimensional aspects of new media influence. If a medium is to help foster change, it need not be overtly political but it must be used creatively and with an understanding of its relationship with other social and political institutions.

Moderation such as Khaled's has its critics. Al-Qaradawi said that Khaled's conciliatory approach during the Danish cartoon controversy of 2006 was a sign of weakness, and the senior cleric contended that Khaled "does not hold any qualifications to preach. He is a business school graduate who acquired what he knows from reading and who got his start by way of conversations with friends about things that do not really involve any particular thought or judgment." Lindsay Wise observed that

> the more Khaled reaches out to the West and America, the more he tries to speak a language that makes everybody happy, the more he risks losing credibility among Arab and Muslim audiences. It is a conundrum familiar to liberal-minded politicians and reformers in the Arab world—a rhetoric of dialogue and conciliation can be a hard sell at times of frustration and conflict.[44]

To some extent, the tension between al-Qaradawi and Khaled reflects what may be called "the Islamic divide" between traditionalists and modernists. As global mass media reach an ever-expanding number of Muslims worldwide, aspirations and expectations among these people may change based on what they receive from satellite television and the Internet. That is not to say that they are going to turn their backs on the tenets of Islam, but rather that they will look for ways to be part of the larger global community, enjoying more of its benefits while retaining their commitment to Islamic principles.

In the context of terrorism, extremists embrace the traditionalist outlook and relish the notion of religious commitment being a facet of the "clash" theory. As the U.S. Combating Terrorism Center reported, "The Jihadi cause is best served when the conflict with local and foreign governments is portrayed as a conflict between Islam and the West. Islam is under siege and only the Jihadis can lift it."[45] Among the media-savvy imams taking advantage of this has been Anwar al-Awlaki, who was implicated in a murderous rampage at Fort Hood, Texas, in which 13 people were killed and 30 others wounded, and the attempt to firebomb an American airliner en route from Amsterdam to Detroit. In terms of audience size, al-Awlaki cannot be compared to the likes of al-Qaradawi or Khaled. But al-Awlaki can reach the audience he wants—those whose perverted sense of jihad may lead them to commit terrorist acts. Al-Awlaki is the post-Zarqawi media master, relying on YouTube to deliver, in Arabic and English, his soft-spoken incitement to violence.

The decline of the gatekeeper

The relationship between religion and media illustrates the essential role of satellite television and the Internet in delivering an unfiltered message to targeted publics. Through new communication technologies, the news media as gatekeeper can be more easily circumvented. This is significant because traditionally the dominant mainstream news organizations have performed a de facto censorship role, deciding when to refuse to deliver to the public material that was, in their judgment, too graphic, too speculative, or too inflammatory. This has sometimes amounted to information paternalism, as when words and images about wartime casualties have been sanitized to conform to perceived public sensitivities.

When the news was about terrorism, this gatekeeping function sometimes kept material such as videos of hostages from reaching the public. If terrorists wanted to communicate with a large public, they could be stymied, at least temporarily, by news organizations. It didn't take long, however, for terrorist strategists to figure out a way around this. If they faced a news blackout, they could escalate their tactics to a level at which the mainstream news media had to cover them. While coverage about the taking of hostages might be withheld (perhaps at a government's request), if the terrorists began executing those hostages, blowing up airplanes, or engaging in other spectacular behavior, the "newsworthiness" of those actions would ensure coverage.

From terrorists' point of view, this comes back to a simple formulation: If a terrorist act goes unreported to the public, has it really happened? The answer is yes for those directly affected by the act, but no, in terms "terrorizing" the larger public. No matter how bloody they may be, terrorist acts are largely symbolic, and for that symbolism to have effect, news of the acts must be communicated. The idea is to wear down the public's commitment to government policies that the terrorists want to see undone. The calculation by bin Laden and some others may be something like this: how many attacks on the United States will it take for the American public to decide that U.S. support of Israel is not worth the cost being paid?

In the context of the public's awareness of terrorism, the rise of new media has rendered obsolete a substantial part of the news media's gatekeeping role. If, for example, news organizations will not show video of a hostage, and particularly not of a hostage being executed, the terrorists can simply post the video on the Web. There it will attract tens of thousands of viewers, and perhaps many more, almost instantly.

With that in mind, news organizations may find themselves reconsidering their standards. If the material is available online and people are going to those sites, should the news media continue to treat their own audiences as if the material doesn't exist? An instructive example (although outside the scope of terrorist fare): When Saddam Hussein was executed in 2006, graphic video of the hanging was surreptitiously captured on a cell phone by someone present. On grounds of taste, most major broadcast news organizations did not show these images. But the footage spread virally across the Internet within hours, attracting 13 million hits just on YouTube, Google Video, and Break.com.[46]

Given how many people were looking at the video, did it still make sense for mainstream news to suppress it, or was that now a pointless exercise? Would making it available to an even larger, "mainstream" audience (whatever that is now) mean surrendering values and letting the marketplace dictate standards?

Similar questions have arisen about terrorist actions such as the filmed execution in 2002 of American journalist Daniel Pearl. The video could be easily found on the Internet, but should mere availability be the determinative factor in shaping journalistic norms?

A related factor is the rise of the "citizen journalist." Video, voice. and text reporting from the scene of a terrorist attack makes the presence of conventional journalists less essential. During the Mumbai attacks in 2008, people trapped inside the Taj hotel transmitted video to news organizations and others from their cell phones and communicated with journalists through text messages. People in the streets outside the hotel posted images from the scene on their Flickr streams. It is hard to imagine a terrorist act that would not be "covered" today, regardless of the ability of traditional media to get to the scene and transmit their reports. During the aftermath of the Mumbai attacks, CNN's license to transmit live video in India expired and it had to rely on telephone reports and footage from Indian channels.[47] Ways can be found around that kind of disruption, and as the amount of citizen journalism from an event reaches a critical mass, major "legacy" news organizations may find themselves following the news flow rather than leading it.

Major terrorist organizations are well aware of the new ways of reaching vast audiences through Internet-based venues and the resulting pressure on conventional media outlets. Those combating terrorism have no choice but to deal with this in a variety of ways that will be examined throughout this book.

Online radicalization

If terrorism is to have effect, it must be communicated. If terrorism is to be sustained, it must recruit new adherents. Once the stories of terrorist activity reach the general public, organizations such as Al Qaeda try to capitalize on the publicity in their recruitment efforts. Online venues are particularly important in this work.

In the United States, the 2006 National Intelligence Estimate reported that "the radicalization process is occurring more quickly, more widely, and more anonymously in the Internet age, raising the likelihood of surprise attacks by unknown groups whose members and supporters may be difficult to pinpoint."[48]

Marc Sageman noted in 2008 that "the pre-9/11 Al Qaeda terrorists were radicalized through face-to-face interaction," but that this has been replaced by online radicalization. He stated:

> It is the interactivity of the group that changes people's beliefs, and such interaction is found in Islamist extremist forums on the Internet. The same support and validation that young people used to derive from their offline peer groups are now found in these forums, which promote the image of terrorist heroes, link them to the virtual social movement, give them guidance, and instruct them in tactics. These forums, virtual

marketplaces for extremist ideas, have become the virtual "invisible hand" organizing terrorist activities worldwide. The true leader of this social movement is the collective discourse on a half dozen influential forums. They are transforming the terrorist movement, recruiting ever younger members and now more prominently women, who can participate in the discussions.[49]

Given the dispersal of information distribution, principally through online venues, the "cascade" model designed by Robert Entman becomes more complex. In addition to the flow from government and elites through the framing process by traditional media entities, certain information may also flow through extremist information providers and acquire a wholly different frame. Steven Corman, Angela Trethewey, and H. L. Goodall, Jr. have used coverage of the 2006 death of Abu Musab al-Zarqawi to illustrate this alternative path: information released, in this case, by American officials, passing through extremist Web sites, the framing of martyrdom (as opposed to the welcomed death of a terrorist), and the response by a targeted public that accepts the martyrdom frame. These scholars wrote that the Web sites and bloggers see and interpret the news in different ways, but

> how they see and interpret the information is beyond the control of Western media elites and their spokespersons. In the case of the circulation of the death images of Zarqawi, it was the release and circulation of those images that led to his death being framed as worthy of martyrdom.

They added that in the Zarqawi example

> the photographic information presented in a military press conference is the exact same photographic information that appears on a Jihadi Web site, but the interpretation of its meaning is entirely dependent upon the local framing of the image within a specific cultural and political environment.[50]

In one venue, it is proof that an evil man is dead. In other venues, it is evidence of a hero attaining glorious martyrdom and its rewards.

Online radicalization works well with the network structure of many terrorist groups. Gabriel Weimann has written that Al Qaeda and other such groups

> are loosely organized networks that rely less on hierarchical structure and more on horizontal networking. To varying degrees, many modern terrorist groups share the pattern of the loosely knit network: decentralization, segmentation, and delegation of authority. These features of postmodern terrorism make computer-mediated communication an ideal tool of coordination, information exchange, training, and recruitment.[51]

The Internet allows fast and inexpensive dissemination of even complex information to diverse constituencies, ranging from the potential recruit to prospective partners in terrorist enterprises.

In the next chapter, in which Al Qaeda is prominently featured, the use of online technologies in the work of terrorist organizations is described in greater detail.

2 High tech terror

Al Qaeda and beyond

At the heart of discussions about contemporary terrorism is Al Qaeda. As an organization it is not fully understood, and analysis of its strength and the nature of its structure vary greatly. Despite this uncertainty, questions about dealing with Al Qaeda preoccupy policymakers in many countries around the world.

Although other extremist groups may embrace violence for reasons of their own, Al Qaeda's high-profile operations, particularly the 2001 attacks on the United States and later attacks in Great Britain and Spain, have made it something of an exemplar in the world of terrorism, particularly because of the extensive media coverage it has received. As such, it provides a useful starting point for contemplating the reach and methods of a diverse array of terrorist enterprises.

Understanding Al Qaeda

Al Qaeda's history and is leadership have been thoroughly examined elsewhere, in volumes such as Lawrence Wright's superb *The Looming Tower*, the writings of Peter Bergen, Abdel Bari Atwan, Jason Burke, and many others. Therefore, no need exists to duplicate that historical analysis here. For the purposes of this book, however, it is useful to assess the state of Al Qaeda in the decade following the 9/11 attacks on the United States.

"Defeat Al Qaeda" remains a mantra among American counterterrorism officials and their counterparts in the United Kingdom, Germany, and elsewhere. That sounds straightforward, but what does it really mean? What exactly is "Al Qaeda" and how does one "defeat" it? This question resonates when contemplating strategies to follow in a "war on terror." How does one wage war against a concept, even if that concept generates physical acts?

First, the threat posed by Al Qaeda and like-minded groups must be treated as being very real, regardless of the amounts of time that may pass between attacks. Al Qaeda envisions its struggle as extending far into an indefinite future. Although Al Qaeda's schedule may be a mystery, the casualty figures from attacks in Nairobi, New York and Washington, Riyadh, Madrid, London, and elsewhere underscore the menace of Osama bin Laden's organization and its affiliates, however loosely connected they might be. The Al Qaeda brand is used by groups that presumably have no contact with one another, such as Al Qaeda in the Arabian Peninsula, Al Qaeda in the Islamic Maghreb, and others. Al Qaeda ventures range from the carefully planned, such as the 2001 attacks on the United States, to the offhand opportunistic incidents such as the attempted firebombing of an American airliner in 2009.

Whatever the level of the attacks, no state can tolerate such belligerent acts being directed against it, although debate continues about whether the response to such actions should be mainly military or instead rely on a police-plus-diplomacy strategy.

Once the threat is acknowledged and the decision to respond is made, the next steps are difficult. The U.S. invasion of Afghanistan in 2001 was a rare—perhaps unique—instance of being able to confront Al Qaeda (and its Taliban allies) on a conventional battlefield. If "defeating Al Qaeda" was a task that could be fully undertaken in that context, the military capabilities of the United States and its allies would undoubtedly prevail. But Al Qaeda is not an "army" in a traditional sense, as its defeat in Afghanistan reminded its leaders. It is not even an "organization" in the usual meaning of that word; it is primarily a virtual entity that exists everywhere and nowhere, an idea as much as a substantive presence.

In an evaluation of Al Qaeda's status in mid-2008, the *Economist* noted that "Al Qaeda is a terrorist organization, a militant network, and a subculture of rebellion all at the same time." Although it does have a physical presence in Pakistan, Somalia, and other places, the article posits that it also is a

"virtual caliphate" of cyberspace. The Internet binds together the amorphous cloud of jihadist groups, spreads the ideology, weaves together the "single narrative" that Islam is under attack, popularizes militant acts, and distributes terrorist know-how. Because Al Qaeda is so dispersed, the fight against it has strained an international order still based on sovereign states.[1]

This issue was raised in *The 9/11 Commission Report*:

National security used to be considered by studying foreign frontiers, weighing opposing groups of states, and measuring industrial might. To be dangerous, an enemy had to muster large armies. Threats emerged slowly, often visibly, as weapons were forged, armies conscripted, and units trained and moved into place. Because large states were so powerful, they also had more to lose. They could be deterred. Now threats can emerge quickly. An organization like Al Qaeda, headquartered in a country on the other side of the earth, in a region so poor that electricity or telephones were scarce, could nonetheless scheme to wield weapons of unprecedented destructive power in the largest cities of the United States.[2]

This point underscores that the shift from both the strategic capabilities and the mentality used in fighting the twentieth century's wars has been awkward. The United States and other major powers had become muscle-bound—able to deter and, presumably, crush opponents of nearly equal stature, but unable to adapt to the pinpoint microwarfare needed in dealing with terrorists.

Similarly, adjusting to the concept that leaders of the enemy are not the leaders of states has been difficult. Determining the roles of Osama bin Laden and Ayman al-Zawahiri is an adjunct to understanding what Al Qaeda is. Some experts, such as Marc Sageman, see terrorism as principally a realm of independent operators who look for targets of opportunity rather than being coordinated as part of a grand strategy.[3] For these perpetrators, bin Laden and Zawahiri are remote symbolic figures whom they might admire but do not truly follow. This view is countered by other experts, such as Jonathan Evans, head of Britain's MI5, who said in 2007 that terrorist efforts in Britain "are not simply random plots by disparate and fragmented groups," but rather "have taken place because Al Qaeda has a clear determination to mount terrorist attacks against the United Kingdom."[4] According to this theory, bin Laden, in particular, is an inspirational figure whose grand strategy is the foundation for operational initiatives that at the very least receive impetus from an Al Qaeda chain of command.

Al Qaeda's intentions are not a mystery. Ample documentation exists, in the form of public pronouncements and more substantial writings, particularly from bin Laden and Zawahiri, about Al Qaeda's rationale and plans. They are laid out and updated in a variety of online forums and publications, offering a "transparency" that may seem to contradict the principles of secrecy that one would assume would be embraced by terrorist organizations. Peter Bergen has observed,

> As we have learned to our cost in recent years, much "secret" information is simply wrong, while information that is public—for instance, bin Laden's repeated calls for attacks against the United States in the years before 2001—is too often discounted.[5]

Perhaps U.S. policymakers would have been more alert to the possibility of these attacks and also would have been wary about venturing into Iraq if they had studied Al Qaeda's pronouncements. They might also have recognized that part of Al Qaeda's strategy related to attacking the United States was to "provoke and bait" American troops into "bleeding wars" in Muslim nations, a move certain to be an invaluable recruitment tool for terrorist groups while proving a politically untenable position for Al Qaeda's enemies.[6]

Despite the useful presence of these "infidel crusaders," Al Qaeda is not immune from pushback from among its own presumed constituencies. Among the events most damaging to Al Qaeda was a series of bombings in Amman, Jordan in November 2005, orchestrated by Abu Musab al-Zarqawi, leader of Al Qaeda in Iraq. The blasts killed dozens, almost all of whom were

Muslim, including members of a wedding party. Jordanians then held rallies condemning Zarqawi. Others in Al Qaeda warned him about the harm he was doing to the cause.

Even more damaging to Al Qaeda over a longer term have been the commentaries of Sayyid Imam al-Sharif, a founder of Al Qaeda in the 1980s, who writes from an Egyptian jail under the pen name of Dr. Fadl. He condemned the 9/11 attacks, calling them "a catastrophe for Muslims ... What good is it if you destroy one of your enemy's buildings and he destroys one of your countries?" He also wrote, "There is nothing that invokes the anger of God and His wrath like the unwarranted spilling of blood and wrecking of property."[7] This line of criticism, based on Islamic theological grounds, reflects broader opposition to Al Qaeda from Muslims who do not consider their religion to be one of violence.

Al-Sharif's recent writings have had significant impact because of his own history. In 1988, he published *The Essential Guide for Preparation,* in which he defined jihad as requiring martyrdom and eternal warfare. He followed this in 1989 with *The Compendium of the Pursuit of Divine Knowledge* that stated that anyone who voted in an election or otherwise participated in a government that did not operate under sharia was an apostate who should be killed. In the 1990s, he began to change his outlook, adopting the position that haphazard use of violence—particularly the killing of Muslims—was contrary to principles of Islamic law. This put him directly at odds with the Al Qaeda leadership, and his writings are now widely distributed on line by the Egyptian government (which as of early 2010 still held him in prison) and others who support radical change but without violence.

Despite such criticism, Al Qaeda has proved resilient and persistent, even while enduring questions about its capabilities and increasingly sophisticated military targeting of its leadership. A spate of "whatever happened to Al Qaeda" articles appear in the news media whenever bin Laden is quiet for a prolonged period, and the public in the West may think the terrorist threat has withered. That is based more on wishful thinking than on hard evidence. The importance of bin Laden himself is overrated because of Western news media's constant search for a "star" around whom to build their coverage. The dispersed and relatively autonomous nature of Al Qaeda as a global presence means that bin Laden is more a symbolic figure than a hands-on director of operations.

It is important to remember that Al Qaeda's sense of time does not conform to that of the "breaking news" society in which if something does not happen quickly it will not happen at all. In early 2009, bin Laden proclaimed that his followers would "continue jihad for another seven years, seven more after that, and even seven more after."[8]

Into the caves and onto the Web

When Al Qaeda was being driven out of Afghanistan in 2001, an observer watched as what seemed to be every other Al Qaeda member carried a laptop computer along with his Kalashnikov.[9] Osama bin Laden and what was left of Al Qaeda moved into the caves of northwestern Pakistan, and the action shifted from a conventional battleground (where Al Qaeda and the Taliban could not compete with U.S. military power) to a virtual one.

Internet use linked to Al Qaeda had begun several years before. In 1996, an undergraduate at Imperial College in London, Babar Ahmad, created azzam. com, named in honor of Abdullah Azzam, a Palestinian who was a mentor to bin Laden and had persuaded bin Laden to come to Afghanistan in the 1980s. The English-language site provided reports about jihad and mujahideen from Chechnya and, beginning in November 2001, Afghanistan. Given the dearth of information emanating from that part of the world, its coverage was sometimes cited by news organizations such as the BBC. The technically sophisticated site provided a forum for teaching a global audience about jihad and built the foundation for a network by providing links to other, like-minded sites.[10]

Al Qaeda soon adopted the Internet as the best medium for sending and receiving messages to scattered audiences. The Al Neda Web site, which Al Qaeda began using in early 2002, published analyses of the wars in Afghanistan and Iraq, commentary by Islamic clerics about Al Qaeda operations, and explanations of how Al Qaeda's war aims would benefit the *ummah* (the global community of Islam) by undermining the power of the United States, Israel, and apostate governments of Muslim states. The content of Al Qaeda-related sites, wrote Michael Scheuer, "adds up to a tremendous contribution to what bin Laden always has said is his and al Qaeda's first priority: the instigation to jihad of as many Muslims in as many locales as possible."[11]

Al Qaeda's Internet operations gradually became more sophisticated and secure. According to a 2004 report by the U.S. Justice and Treasury Departments, the traditional espionage communication technique of the "dead drop" was adapted for online use. Selected Al Qaeda members are given the same prearranged username and password for an e-mail account such as at hotmail.com. One person writes a message, but instead of sending it he saves it in the "draft" file and signs off. Then someone else can access the account, read the message, and either leave it for someone else to read or delete it. Because the message was never sent, the ISP retains no copy of it, and no record of it traversing the Internet exists.[12] A similarly useful tool is the discussion board, where announcements can be posted with links to dozens of sites.

While devising secure methods of communicating, Al Qaeda was also amassing an online library of training materials that would teach its readers how to make ricin poison, how to make a bomb from commercial chemicals, and other useful advice. The Saudi-based online magazine *Muaskar al-Battar* (Camp of the Sword) told potential recruits, "Oh, Mujahid brother, in order to join the great training camps you don't have to travel to other lands. Alone in your home or with a group of your brothers you too can begin to execute the training program." Such training efforts can reach many people quickly and avoid the dangers of recruits gathering at a mosque or other place where they might be observed. John Arquilla has noted that Al Qaeda appreciates that "both time and space have in many ways been conquered by the Internet," and Bruce Hoffman has commented that the Internet offers Al Qaeda a "virtual sanctuary" because it is "the ideal medium for terrorism today: anonymous but pervasive."[13]

The Al Qaeda-affiliated Global Islamic Media Front, primarily serving sympathizers living in Europe, is among the providers that have featured online videos (of good production quality) showing how to plan a roadside assassination, fire a rocket-propelled grenade and a surface-to-air missile, blow up a car, take hostages, and employ other tactics.[14]

As well as providing instruction, Al Qaeda's online material urges its readers to rally to the cause. *Sawt al-Jihad* (Voice of Jihad) is an online magazine that first appeared in 2004 to tout the accomplishments of mujahedin. Its tone is illustrated by this excerpt from an October 2004 editorial:

> Muslims! Go out to [fight] Jihad for the sake of Allah! Paradise has already flung open its gates and the virgins of paradise are already decked out in anticipation of their grooms—this is Allah's promise. He [Allah] will not grant peace of mind to anyone who has a heart until he has gone out to fight against Allah's enemies, as he was commanded.[15]

While proselytizing in such ways, the online magazines also remind readers of the importance of cybersecurity. The online *Technical Mujahid Magazine* was begun in late 2006 to instruct its readers about electronic data security and other high-tech matters. Despite the need for caution, Al Qaeda has used its Web sites to urge its followers to make full use of the Internet. This message was on one of the sites:

> We strongly urge Muslim Internet professionals to spread and disseminate news and information about the Jihad through e-mail lists, discussion groups, and their own Web sites. If you fail to do this, and our site closes down before you have done this, we may hold you to account before Allah on the Day of Judgment. ... We expect our Web site to be opened and closed continuously. Therefore we urgently recommend any Muslims that are interested in our material to copy all the articles from our site and disseminate them through their own Web sites, discussion boards, and e-mail lists. This is something that any Muslim can participate in easily, including sisters. This way, even if our sites are closed down, the material will live on with the Grace of Allah.[16]

By relying heavily on its Internet capabilities, Al Qaeda has rendered moot some of the questions about its structure. Neither the "leaderless jihad" concept articulated by Marc Sageman nor the view of Bruce Hoffman that Al Qaeda is alive and well can be proved fully. Peter Bergen has argued that, "Al Qaeda as an organization is severely impaired, but it has been replaced by a broader ideological movement made up of self-starting, homegrown terrorists who have few formal links to Al Qaeda but are motivated by a doctrine that can be called "Binladenism."[17] On the other side of the spectrum is the opinion reported by Craig Whitlock in 2007 that

> today, Al Qaeda operates much the way it did before 2001. The network is governed by a shura, or leadership council, that meets regularly and reports to bin Laden, who continues to approve some major decisions, according to a senior U.S. intelligence official. About 200 people belong to the core group and many receive regular salaries, another senior U.S. intelligence official said. "They do appear to meet with a frequency that enables them to act as an organization and not just as a loose bunch of guys," the second official said.[18]

Whichever point of view is accepted about the status of Al Qaeda per se, there is agreement among those who best understand terrorist operations that defenses against terrorism should not be relaxed. Unless all the Al Qaeda-related Internet content has no one behind it who is willing to act—which is not provable, the assumption must be that a real threat exists. The scenario that Al Qaeda is on the run and is in shambles, and has lost its appeal to the greater Muslim community, is supported by some survey research and is certainly enticing. But to accept that theory and relax would be courting trouble, possibly at a disastrous level.

Osama bin Laden's principal deputy, Ayman al-Zawahiri, has been a leading proponent of Al Qaeda's use of "Jihadi information media" in "waging an extremely critical battle against the Crusader-Zionist enemy."[19] Zawahiri's pronouncements, which appear frequently online, are worth noting because they indicate not only that he is alive and stirring the embers of Al Qaeda's fire, but also that Al Qaeda's list of opponents within the Muslim world has expanded. In two appearances in December 2007, one a video and the other an audio recording, he accused Iran of cooperating with the United States in Iraq and Afghanistan and said Al Qaeda would not aid Iran in the event of an attack by U.S. forces. "Iran has stabbed a knife into the back of the Islamic nation," he said, "and the traces of this stabbing will remain in the Muslim memory for a long time to come." In the same video, Zawahiri accused Hassan Nasrallah, secretary-general of Hezbollah, of not supporting jihad to liberate Muslim lands but rather representing a "narrow, fanatical nationalist perception" of jihad. Zawahiri went on to also criticize Hamas, urging the Palestinian organization to abandon diplomacy and to instead

> aspire to implement shar'ia, that you reject the rule of the masses and any other rule except that of the Koran and the Sunna, that you strive to establish the Caliphate ... that you aspire to liberate every inch of Islamic land from Andalusia to Chechnya ... I call upon you to announce that you are no longer a national resistance movement, but an Islamic jihad movement

which transcends national solidarity and believes in brotherhood rooted in Islam.

Finally, Zawahiri asked Egyptians, "How did you allow Egypt to become a support base for the Crusader campaign against the Muslims? Beware the poison of weakness and submissiveness that the collaborating regimes are attempting to spread among you."[20]

That is quite a list of complaints, and it shows the distance between Al Qaeda and Nasrallah, arguably one of the most powerful and popular figures in the more extreme politics of the Middle East. It also indicates tensions between Al Qaeda and Hamas, generally considered a primary champion of Palestinians. The audience supporting such positions must be tiny; it is unreasonable to expect significant defections from Hezbollah or Hamas because of such exhortations. Perhaps Zawahiri's arguments are well received by a small but potent group of purists in the Arab world and beyond. Not many committed people are needed to conduct terrorist operations, and maybe Zawahiri was trying to rally this resolute core.

Such messages also provide insight into how Al Qaeda defines itself and its jihadist struggle. The traditional nation-state in the Muslim world is seen as an anachronism that serves the interest of infidels and their lackeys, and so even changes of government that lead to shar'ia-based theocracies would be acceptable only temporarily as stepping-stones toward a new caliphate. The constituency for this agenda is, presumably, very small, particularly when taking account of the amount of bloodshed that would accompany it. Al Qaeda has, in effect, marginalized itself, which is something that anti-Al Qaeda public diplomacy might take better advantage of.

Whatever the true back story behind Zawahiri's speeches might be, one can see why counterterrorism officials are among those who prefer that Al Qaeda not be driven entirely off the Internet, which is a rich source of open source intelligence. Of course, Al Qaeda leaders understand this and may be using their online content for disinformation purposes, necessitating skepticism about all messages from Al Qaeda and like groups. Nothing is certain in this wilderness of mirrors.

What *is* certain is that Al Qaeda's aspirations are grounded in hard-nosed realism. Bin Laden and Zawahiri recognize that, in the words of Faisal Devji, "The jihad, like other global movements after the Cold War, is non-geographical in nature, using the most disparate territories as temporary bases for its action. This makes it into an impossible enemy for the United States, because it exists beyond America's war-making potential." It is a new global category "with the geographical, financial, and technological mobility that defines globalization itself."[21] In the first issue (February 2004) of Al Qaeda's online magazine *Sawt al-Jihad* (Voice of the Jihad), Al Qaeda's objectives were defined, writes Gabriel Weimann: "Orchestrating attacks against Western targets is important, but the main objective remains that of mobilizing public support and gaining grassroots legitimacy among Muslims."[22]

The core of that support derives from the mujahideen's success against the Soviet Union in Afghanistan. Of this, Zawahiri has written:

> The USSR, a superpower with the largest land army in the world, was destroyed and the remnants of its troops fled Afghanistan before the eyes of the Muslim youths and as a result of their actions. ... It gave young Muslim mujahidin—Arabs, Pakistanis, Turks, and Muslims from Central and East Asia—a great opportunity to get acquainted with each other on the land of Afghan jihad through their comradeship-at-arms against the enemies of Islam.[23]

Zawahiri's point is valid; pushing the Soviets out of Afghanistan gave the mujahideen credibility that continues today in the Muslim world and beyond, and that was increased by the attacks on the United States, Britain, and Spain.

The Al Qaeda leadership's realism about organizational issues extends to financial matters. Operational budgets are small. The 2001 attacks on the United States are estimated to have cost US$500,000 to plan and execute, the 2005 bombings in London US$15,000, and easily available material to blow up an airliner can be had for about US$15.[24] This is important because the notion of drying up Al Qaeda's funding, a key part of Western counterterrorism plans, may be overrated and, given the minimal costs of attacks to date, unrealistic. As for communicating its message to its followers and the larger world, Al Qaeda needs little funding to sustain its online operations.

Emerging from all these factors is a political stance that combines menace with bravado. By summer 2009, Zawahiri was taking on Barack Obama. In an interview posted on the Internet, Zawahiri said:

> We are not a nation of stupid, gullible people who would let Obama treat us as fools with meaningless, malleable expressions, while he is a new manifestation of the same old American criminality, whose purpose is the implementation of a Zionist scheme. ... The bombardment of the tribal areas [of Pakistan] only increases the hatred of the Muslims toward America, reveals the Pakistani regime's collaboration with the Crusaders, proves that Obama was lying when he said he was beginning a new policy vis-à-vis the Islamic world, and shows that Obama is no more than a shedder of Muslim blood—just like his predecessor, Bush.[25]

Same song, new verse. The defensive, negative tone of such commentary, particularly when coupled with the nihilistic tactics that Bin Laden, Zawahiri, and their coterie embrace, leaves Al Qaeda as a vehicle for expression of rage, but little else. Obama's outreach to the Muslim world, particularly through his visits to Turkey and Egypt early in his presidency, showed that he would compete with Zawahiri et al. for public support. If the number and intensity of grievances of many in the Muslim world could be reduced, Al Qaeda's standing would suffer, despite its image as a fearsome combatant with global reach. There must always be an enemy, and much of the Al Qaeda online product is designed to stir the hatred that sustains extremists. Those nations that are Al Qaeda's targets, such as the United States, seem slow to recognize this, as evidenced by the paltry volume and unimaginative content of their counterprogramming.

Al Qaeda's viability rests largely with its ability to find local partners, which it does by offering its brand name and, more substantively, training, military expertise, some financial help, and media services.[26] This is Al Qaeda as a network, with different levels of connectivity and varied prospects for long-term success or even long-term existence.

Communication strategies

In 2005, Ayman al-Zawahiri wrote to the head of Al Qaeda in Iraq, Abu Musab al-Zarqawi, and stated: "We are in a battle, and more than half of this battle is taking place in the battlefield of the media. We are in a media battle for the hearts and minds of our *ummah*."[27]

The media battle that Zawahiri addressed has been fought with considerable sophistication by Al Qaeda, sustaining a global public presence even when the Al Qaeda leadership has been more or less driven to cover. Osama bin Laden created an Al Qaeda media department in 1988 as part of the group's original organizational structure. The theme of its earliest products was to lionize the mujahideen in Afghanistan who were fighting the Soviet Union, but soon the message shifted to attacking Israel, the United States, and some Arab regimes, particularly Saudi Arabia. By the time bin Laden issued his "Declaration of War on the United States" in 1996, Al Qaeda had embraced "armed defensive jihad." After defeats of Arab armies by Israel and defeats suffered by Pakistan at the hands of India, the Al Qaeda effort was designed partly to restore Muslims' self-respect by increasing their military capabilities, with the ultimate target being the superpower, the United States. During the next decade, primarily by using the Internet, Al Qaeda worked to give Muslims throughout the world a new media option that would be far different than the news products from Western providers such as CNN and the BBC, and even from Arab channels such as Al Jazeera and Al Arabiya.[28]

Al Qaeda designed its own media production operation, As Sahab (The Clouds), to function under tight security requirements. A video of bin Laden, Zawahiri, or other Al Qaeda spokespersons is shot in a remote location, hand-carried to a place where it is safe to upload it to the Internet, and then sent to As Sahab's post-production facility, where it is edited and dressed up with graphics and subtitles. As Sahab reportedly uses first-class equipment (such as Sony Vaio laptops) and Pretty Good Privacy encryption software. The final video product is then put on a memory stick, taken by a courier to an Internet café, and uploaded to various Al Qaeda-affiliated Web sites. The addresses of these sites are then published in Internet forums and chat rooms. Then Al Qaeda followers copy and further distribute the video. This system has been used since 2005, when Al Qaeda stopped delivering videotapes to Al Jazeera and other news organizations, which would edit them as they chose, sometimes diminishing the intended impact of the material.[29]

In 2005, As Sahab released 16 videos. By 2007, the number had reached 97 original productions. By 2009, As Sahab was distributing videos showing Americans under attack in Afghanistan, posting videos in Urdu, and presenting a documentary series, "The Protectors of the Sanctuary," with 40-minute tributes to Al Qaeda supporters who had been killed.[30] The best-known of the As Sahab videos are those featuring bin Laden, who has said that 90 percent of his efforts are carried out through the media. Since the 9/11 attacks, he has issued more than two dozen videos and audiotapes in which he has called for attacks on Westerners and Jews, and sometimes has issued more specific instructions, such as for attacks in Pakistan. This may be one reason for the increase in suicide bombings in that country beginning in 2007.[31]

In addition to As Sahab, Al Qaeda has a media distribution and "public relations" arm called the Global Islamic Media Front. Among its products was a 2006 "Working Paper for a Media Invasion of America," written by Al Qaeda ally Najd al-Rawi, who apparently was inspired by a bin Laden video with subtitles in English. The working paper calls for enlistment in the Al Qaeda cause by translators and people with journalistic talent and computer expertise who can provide a "ringing and powerful style that will have impact on the American people." Proposed projects included translations of pronouncements by Al Qaeda leaders such as "Sharia rules regarding the use of WMDs," which presumably would "throw fear into the American people's hearts." The paper also suggests feeding such material to Internet discussion forums and chat rooms, as well as providing it to well-known news organizations and writers.[32]

Al Qaeda's offshoots do not use As Sahab but have their own media operations. Al Qaeda in the Islamic Maghreb released a video of a 2006 attack on Halliburton subsidiary Brown & Root-Condor in Algeria. AQIM has also produced videos showing its attacks on Algerian military convoys and bombings in Algiers.[33] In Somalia, Al Shabab announced in late 2009 that it had established its own media company, Al Kataib, as its exclusive provider of information about the organization. The Al Shabab announcement said in part:

> In light of the media blackout on the affairs and the victories of the jihad fighters, and the brutal attacks on their reputation ... it has become imperative to form media companies affiliated with the jihad and muja-hideen. Despite the shortage of experts in this field, we managed, with Allah's help, to enter the media domain and gain a firm foothold in it.[34]

As Al Qaeda's global connections have grown, As Sahab has been supplemented by Al Fajr (The Dawn), which distributes online products to Web-masters around the world. Content has come from Al Qaeda affiliates in Iraq,

Yemen, Somalia, and North Africa, as well as from the Taliban and other such groups. The material is often subtitled in English, German, Italian, French, Pashto, Turkish and other languages. Al Fajr is decentralized; the Web-masters do not work with one another. The operation has subgroups assigned to hacking, multimedia, cybersecurity, and distribution. Release of new material is announced on password-protected Web forums.[35]

Al Fajr's operations demonstrate two levels of the sophistication of Al Qaeda and related groups. First, security is comprehensive and sophisticated. People in the communication network are well protected and the system is designed to prevent distribution of planted disinformation. Second, and more important, Al Fajr illustrates Al Qaeda's flexible and pervasive global structure. By resisting the temptation to create a worldwide "organization" with precisely defined hierarchies and rigid construction, Al Qaeda is able to advance its goals while remaining amorphous enough to foil attempts to attack or penetrate it.

The Internet is a perfect tool for Al Qaeda. By operating online, Al Qaeda can keep multiple operations going, disseminate a multitude of products, and advance its operational goals with relatively little expense and little risk. One Al Qaeda spokesman has referred to the Internet as the "Al Qaeda University of Jihad Studies."[36]

This "university" offers a range of educational aids that reflect Al Qaeda strategist Abu Mus'ab al-Suri's theory that training should be a global enterprise. In his 1,600-page treatise *The Global Islamic Resistance Call* (2005), al-Suri wrote that rather than bringing recruits to Afghanistan or other Al Qaeda strongholds, "it is necessary to move training to every house, every quarter, and every village of the Muslim countries." He added that Al Qaeda needed "the spread of a culture of preparation and training by all methods, especially the Internet."[37]

Al-Suri's position, however, has not been uniformly embraced within Al Qaeda. Anne Stenersen of the Norwegian Research Defense Establishment wrote that "as of today [2008], the Internet is not a 'virtual training camp' organized from above, but rather a resource bank maintained and accessed largely by self-radicalized sympathizers."[38] But even if lacking organization from above, this resource bank provides plenty of information that can lead to lethal results. Perhaps the best-known of the online handbooks is the *Encyclopedia for the Preparation of Jihad*, which was first created during the 1979–89 Afghan-Soviet war. At 700 megabytes (10,000 pages when downloaded), the encyclopedia has been added to and revised frequently and features particular emphasis on homemade explosives. The visitors' count on the Encyclopedia's Web site showed more than 390,000 visits as of mid-2007.[39]

Overall, the Internet primarily provides access to training manuals and some interactive connections with instructors. Sophisticated instructional videos are rare, although some illustrate how to create an explosive belt and work with poisonous gas. Occasionally material related to nuclear weapon construction has appeared, but this has mostly been little more than collections of information in the public domain (including, however, material about constructing a radium-based "dirty bomb"). Similarly, one Al Qaeda-affiliated Web forum offered sniper training in the form of the video *The Ultimate Sniper*, an American-produced video that is available from Amazon and many other sources, which had been changed only by adding Arabic subtitles. Stenersen's study of such online content as presented by a number of sources led her to observe that highest quality instructional material has been offered not by Al Qaeda, but by Hezbollah.[40] Further, online training has its limits. Working with explosives and other delicate tasks require an on-site instructor if the lessons are to produce a useful (and still living) operative.

Training for terrorist attacks is far from the only use of the Internet. In addition to reaching committed extremists, the Web provides an invaluable forum for proselytizing to a diverse global audience. One illustration of the intent to reach a worldwide constituency is the increasing use of English-language material. In July 2009, the Al Mosul Islamic Network released the first issue of *Defenders of the Truth*, described as an "English jihad magazine" that calls for Allah to "destroy the enemies of Islam ... the Jews, Christians, atheists, and the betraying criminals." An editor's note said that *Defenders of the Truth* will educate Muslims about "the war on Islam" and "the treacherous governments of the so-called Muslim countries who bow down to the Christians and the Jews."[41] The English-language content was most frequently used by Iraqi insurgent organizations during the most intense fighting in the Iraq war as they tried to tap into the American public's growing dissatisfaction with the Bush administration's conduct of the war. Targeting American Muslims, many of whom do not speak Arabic, followed a fundamental propaganda strategy used—although not always successfully—in previous wars.

Well over 100 English-language sites deliver militant Islamic content. Some providers of such online material operate not from secret hideouts but in plain sight in the United States. One blogger, Samir Khan, relayed Osama bin Laden's pronouncements, Iraqi insurgents' videos, and links to Al Qaeda-related Web sites from his home in North Carolina. After a story about Khan appeared in the *New York Times*, there were public calls for him to be arrested or at least have his blog shut down. The reason that did not happen to Khan and others who generate similar material is, first, they are not breaking U.S. law. Also, law enforcement agencies think these sites pose little real threat and might provide valuable open source intelligence, and so they should be allowed to function while being closely monitored.[42]

Most of the extremist sites are more conventional in the sense that they emanate from Al Qaeda-affiliated individuals or groups. When Abu Musab al-Zarqawi was leading Al Qaeda in Iraq (he was killed in June 2006 by a U.S. bombing raid), he used the Internet more consistently than any other terrorist figure. His first known online project was *Heroes of Fallujah*, a 2004 video that showed several men planting a roadside bomb and then watching as it blew up an American armored personnel carrier. Another of his products was the online magazine *Zurwat al-Sanam* ("Tip of the Camel's Hump," meaning ideal Islamic practice). The first issue, which appeared in 2005, contained 43 pages, including a denunciation of the recent Iraqi elections as un-Islamic. A few months later, Zarqawi's "information wing" produced *All Religion Will Be for Allah*, a video that presented 46 minutes of war footage and a tribute to suicide bombers. The distribution of this video showcased the terrorists' increasing media sophistication: it appeared on a specially designed Web page with numerous links for people who wanted to watch it in different formats. There was a version for those with a high-speed Internet connection, a simpler version for those using a dial-up connection, an option to use Windows Media or RealPlayer, and a version that could be played on a mobile phone, which was an advanced concept in 2005.[43] This offering of material in multiple formats can be found on numerous Web sites.

Zarqawi was also behind one of the most hideous online video offerings. His organization kidnapped American businessman Nicholas Berg and Zarqawi himself (apparently) beheaded the captive. The video of this murder was posted on the Web on May 11, 2004 and within 24 hours it had been copied onto other sites and downloaded more than 500,000 times.[44] Soon the number of viewers was in the millions.

This incident underscored the value of the Internet to terrorists. Mainstream news organizations would certainly not show such graphic footage to the public, but the Web provided a way for Zarqawi to avoid traditional media filters and deliver whatever images he wanted to a vast audience. Al Jazeera, which bin Laden had used as a stage for his video appearances, would not have run the Berg video. Based on the number of downloads, Zarqawi correctly gauged the ghoulish tastes of the part of the public that he wanted to reach. This is a hard-core audience, not a general one, and Zarqawi had apparently decided that he would play to his strength, those who approved of his methods, rather than soften his appeal to make it more acceptable to a wider audience. In 2005, Zarqawi's media team began presenting regular Internet news broadcasts that were billed as "the sole outlet for mujaheddin media."[45]

In addition to the newscasts, Zarqawi's media operation regularly released brief video clips showing snipers, suicide bombers, and roadside bombs all targeted at Americans in Iraq. In 2004, such clips were compiled in an hour-long video titled "The Winds of Victory," which was disseminated through Zarqawi's media organization and other terrorist Web sites.[46]

In terms of volume and graphic content, Zarqawi was a dominant force for several years in the world of terrorist media. His notoriety was boosted by his online presence, and this helped attract fighters to his ranks in Iraq. But as successful as he appeared to be, within the highest levels of Al Qaeda his blood-soaked methods raised concerns. Bin Laden had called Zarqawi "the prince of Al Qaeda in Iraq," but the "collateral damage" of Zarqawi's forces' bombings and other attacks included many Muslim civilians. Media events such as the Berg execution gave credence to characterizations of Al Qaeda's ranks being populated by thugs rather than heroic freedom fighters. In several letters, Ayman al-Zawahiri urged Zarqawi to reduce indiscriminate bloodshed and avoid the horrific theater of executions on video.[47]

Zarqawi left behind a fervent legion of followers who are anti-Shi'a as well as anti-American, but without his star power and because of the changing military and political situation in Iraq, his followers' media operations became less significant. Nevertheless, the pervasive media presence of Al Qaeda continued to expand, strengthening the internal communications of terrorism even if less noticed by Western news media and the general public.

New media tools continue to appear and extremist groups are quick to take advantage of them. YouTube, LiveLeak, Spike, and other such online video services are particularly handy for reaching a global audience with pronouncements from leaders of terrorist groups, video of attacks, and other content that keeps selected publics aware of terrorist activity. One advantage of such open sources is that viewers do not need to be prompted; if they check the sites periodically they will find the material that its suppliers want them to see. The danger of being detected by counterterrorism agencies is slight. Further, chatrooms and software that allow real-time audio or audio-video communication encourage intensive networking among terrorist group leaders, their followers, and prospective recruits.

More significant in terms of actual terrorist operations is the Internet's value in intelligence-gathering. A tool such as Google Earth can greatly enhance the effectiveness of evaluating targets when planning an attack.[48] In one instance, the media arm of the Algerian Al Qaeda in the Islamic Maghreb documented a 2006 attack on a Brown and Root subsidiary, showing preparation of explosives, physical reconnaissance, electronic reconnaissance through online satellite photography, and the attack itself.[49]

From these many uses of Internet-based media emerges a general portrait of terrorist understanding and appreciation of media as a strategic and tactical tool. In 2005, the Al Qaeda-affiliated Global Islamic Media Front established a Media Jihad Brigade as a way to participate without becoming a conventional combatant. The group's announcement explained that "the media war is an integral part of the war on the battlefield," which could be fought by "a group of Muslims who desire to wage jihad and to bear arms, but until Allah allows them to do so, they take upon themselves to help jihad fighters by toppling the Zionist hegemony over the media."[50]

Part of this "media war" involves using the Internet to attack adversaries' Web sites and to steal sensitive information through electronic break-ins. Extremist Web forums may have sections with instructions about this kind of warfare and calls for recruits to take part in electronic jihad. One such notice in 2005 said: "The largest campaign to destroy Crusader websites: We need mujahideen! The timing of the electronic attack is Thursday at 19:00 GMT. The attack will last for one hour. We have 50 mujahideen so far who are ready for this campaign." These attacks targeted two sites that endorsed Muslim-Christian dialogue.[51]

Such casual online recruiting has been replaced in some instances with a more sophisticated approach. In 2008, an Al Qaeda-related Internet forum featured a new manual titled *The Art of Recruitment*, which recommended a carefully planned one-on-one evaluation and religion-based cultivation of prospects. The final steps in a weeks-long process included "awakening the faith" with the promise of heaven for aggressive jihadis.[52]

The careful recruitment process was designed to ensure quality and protect security. This latter concern is addressed repeatedly on extremist sites. Advice is offered on how to mask a computer's IP address, how to use a proxy server, and other ways to hide online identity. Extremist forum members are also aware that their online activities are being monitored by a large number of intelligence and law enforcement agencies and by private organizations that watch terrorists' online work. In 2008, an Al Qaeda site posted "Know Your Enemy from Monitoring and Analysis Websites," which described specific translation sites, investigative sites, and research projects, as well as news coverage, and made clear that they should be considered tools of the enemy.[53] Anwar al-Awlaki, an American-educated Yemeni imam linked to the murders committed at Fort Hood in 2009, wrote, "The only ones who are spending the money and time translating Jihad literature are the Western intelligence services."[54]

Extremist online forums often contain warnings about intelligence agencies' methods of penetrating communication networks. Technical means include monitoring e-mail traffic to and from a particular address, planting Trojans (which allow unauthorized access) in a target's computer; hacking into a target's computer, and posting material in Web forums while using the target's online nickname. Less technically oriented are psychological ploys such as posting critical items likely to draw a response from a target (such as challenging a Salafist precept), or engaging the target in apparently supportive online communication that may draw him into exposing information about himself or others.[55]

One of these forums addressed dangers awaiting its members who need to pay for products or services. The forum moderator warned about the many ways that using bank transfers of credit cards could be traced by intelligence agencies, and went on to say, "If you have not gotten arrested yet, that does not mean you are not being monitored, and if your use of the electronic payments method has not brought you woes, then that does not mean it is safe."[56]

For security agencies, such efforts might occasionally create a disruption in a part of a terrorist organization, or even lead to an arrest. But such successes are likely to be infrequent, given the Al Qaeda model of dispersed cells and loose connections. Gabriel Weimann has observed:

> In the loose network structure, group members are organized into cells that have little or no contact with other cells or with a central control or headquarters. Leaders do not issue orders to the cells but rather distribute information via the media, Web sites, and e-mails that can be distributed and accessed anonymously. The advantage of this operational structure is that surveillance, penetration, or capture of operatives does not lead the intelligence agency to other cells or to the central control structure.[57]

Espionage novel-style traps are not necessary to find many of the key players in terrorist culture because they operate in the open, carefully keeping within the boundaries of legality while still advancing extremist causes, usually through online media. Anwar al-Awlaki is a good example. Born in New Mexico in 1971 and with degrees from Colorado State University and San Diego State University, Awlaki delivers messages in praise of jihad on his blog, YouTube, CDs, and booklets. He is easy to listen to, speaking in colloquial, American-accented English, with a style that is more conversation than preaching. His notoriety increased in late 2009 after U.S. Army Major Nidal Malik Hassan killed 13 people at Fort Hood, Texas, apparently in reaction to his being ordered to serve in Afghanistan. Hassan had been communicating regularly with Awlaki, seeking religious advice about his military service. Several years previously, terrorists accused of plotting attacks in the United States and Canada were known to have listened to Awlaki's sermons. For Muslim soldiers such as Maj. Hassan, Awlaki raised the question, "What kind of twisted fight is this?" and said that a Muslim who killed other Muslims in combat "is a heartless beast, bent on evil, who sells his religion for a few dollars." After the shootings at Fort Hood, Awlaki called Hassan a hero, writing on his blog, "The only way a Muslim could Islamically justify serving as a soldier in the U.S. Army is if his intention is to follow in the footsteps of Nidal."[58]

Although Awlaki does not mention Osama bin Laden or Al Qaeda, this is the Al Qaeda message, and it illustrates why the media fixation on bin Laden is overdone. Using the Internet, presumably from a haven in Yemen, Awlaki wields significant malignant influence, and there is no reason to assume he is unique or that he has any substantive connection to Al Qaeda. Anyone intellectually adroit enough to develop articulate, malignant messages can selectively reach an audience that includes people needing only a polemical nudge to engage in violence. The Internet helps the audience and the proselytizer to identify each other, and then deliver the message. The process is insidious and defies attempts to stop it.

Some other players

Taliban

Although they condemn television and cinema, the Taliban of Afghanistan have embraced print and radio and recognize the value of new media. They have produced DVDs for recruiting and boosting their fighters' morale. A frequent topic had been the beheading of "spies," but as had been the case in Iraq, public aversion to the beheadings grew and the Taliban leadership gave orders to stop. One Taliban commander told a local news agency, "From now on we will be executing the secret agents by shooting instead of slaughtering them."[59] Instead, the Taliban videos that can be found on YouTube and other sites feature more conventional military action, such as attacks on U.S. military units.

The Taliban has had a Web presence since 2005 under variations of the title "Al Emarah" ("The Emirate"). It is regularly taken down by service providers and then it pops up again, often with the banner in Pashtu, "Da Jihad Ghag" ("Call to Jihad"). The Taliban have their own production capability and this site has maintained sections in Pashtu, Dari, Urdu, Arabic, and English, with the Pashtu section being the most extensive and frequently updated. It does not provide links to other extremist organizations and has not published instruction manuals, but it has featured poetry extolling the Taliban's efforts to reinforce Afghans' pride and anger. The Taliban's online presence has not matched the sophistication of Al Qaeda's Web products.[60] As the number of American combat troops in Afghanistan has increased, the frequency of appearances of Taliban combat videos has likewise grown.

Hizb ut Tahrir

Perhaps no extremist group is more Web-centric than Hizb ut Tahrir (Party of Liberation). Long portraying itself as having an ideological rather than a paramilitary mission, Hizb ut Tahrir has led a shadowy existence that has been tolerated in many Western countries. It endorses the establishment of a world-wide caliphate, and although for a number of years it urged gradual adoption of this principle through political conversion, it has recently become more militant. Concerning the non-Muslim world, Hizb ut Tahrir has embraced the idea of a clash of civilizations, and as a player in the politics of Islam it has benefitted from public dissatisfaction with inept governments and political movements.[61]

Zeyno Baran has observed that "the Internet's global reach is perfect for a group that denies the legitimacy of political borders. [Hizb ut Tahrir's] Web sites can be easily accessed by Muslims anywhere, and the Internet is especially effective at facilitating communications with and among people living in repressive societies. The party has essentially constructed a virtual Islamist community in cyberspace, frequented by members, prospective members, and sympathizers."[62]

Officials of some governments, such as Russia and Bangladesh, have not hesitated to label Hizb ut Tahrir a terrorist organization, while in other countries, such as Britain, government has only gradually moved toward banning the organization. Although Hizb ut Tahrir organizes rallies against the United States and Israel, it has not been directly linked to acts of violence such as suicide bombings, and it remains somewhat elusive politically. It consistently recruits and organizes online but only occasionally becomes visible in the non-virtual world. Its cyber-footprints are often found but are hard to follow.

Fuerzas Armadas Revolucionarias de Colombia (FARC)[63]

FARC is Latin America's oldest insurgency group, coming to life during the 1960s, early in Latin America's Castro era. Although its early communist leanings are less pronounced today, FARC continues to portray itself as a champion of the oppressed poor and an opponent of the influence of the United States. Its 10–15,000 guerrillas have been fighting in the jungles of Colombia since its inception, relying on the recruitment of young people, in some cases children, to fill its ranks. Among its most prominent tactics is kidnapping, with an estimated 800 victims being held as late as 2008 in isolated FARC encampments. Although on the decline due to increased efforts on the part of the Colombian government to eliminate them, FARC forces controlled large portions of Colombia for over 40 years. The United States, the European Union, and others have designated FARC as a terrorist organization. Venezuelan president Hugo Chavez, on the other hand, is among those who consider FARC to be a legitimate revolutionary movement. His stance has kept tensions high between Venezuela and Colombia.

In recent years, FARC has relied on different forms of media to spread its message. The bulk of user-generated, pro-FARC media can be found on You-Tube, with songs glorifying individual members and the struggle in general, and videos depicting armed combat in a positive light. This kind of FARC propaganda reaches a crucial audience—young people and potential recruits. Video clips featuring FARC engaging in armed combat against the backdrop of techno music glorify FARC activities and portray combat as exciting.[64]

There is a plethora of pro-FARC songs on YouTube often used in replies to anti-FARC media. One catchy pro-FARC melody is dedicated to FARC leader Alfonso Cano, and opens with "The struggle is long but we will triumph."[65] The song urges any man who values liberty to take up arms, enlist in the insurgency, and join the Bolivarian struggle.

Despite its longstanding YouTube presence and use of other Web tools, FARC was to learn that the Internet can bite back. In 2008, a Facebook group, "A Million Voices Against FARC," was created by a 33-year-old Colombian engineer, Oscar Morales. Within 24 hours, 3,000 people subscribed. By late 2008, the group had more than 300,000 members. The group's slogan is, "No more! No more kidnapping! No more lies! No more murder! No more FARC!" In February 2008, the group, communicating primarily though Facebook, organized rallies around the world, with events taking place throughout Latin America and in more than 160 cities as far away as Sydney and Paris, with participation estimated to be in the millions. The message delivered by Facebook was, "Let's commit ourselves to join a million voices in this group so we can make a difference, and let the whole world know that FARC is a terrorist group."[66]

Although the anti-FARC effort captured worldwide attention and mostly favorable news coverage, some pushback occurred. Some bloggers commented: "The problem in Colombia is not just FARC. It should not be 'No more FARC.' It should be 'No more war!'" Colombia's Left-leaning Polo Democratico Party did not participate in the Facebook-organized marches, but organized its own rally in Bogota to support negotiations between the government and FARC.[67]

Regardless of the politics surrounding pro- and anti-FARC groups, this is a useful case in terms of illustrating how terrorist (and allegedly terrorist) organizations use new media to sustain themselves and how their opponents use the same media technologies to respond.

Ejercito de Liberacion Nacional (ELN)[68]

The ELN, National Liberation Army, was formed in 1963 by students, Catholics, and left-wing intellectuals. It is considered more ideological than FARC, but both oppose U.S. influence in Colombia and claim to represent the rural poor. The ELN has recently shifted its focus to urban areas. It has operated mainly in northeastern Colombia and has between 2,200 and 3,000 members.[69]

Like FARC, ELN is known for kidnapping wealthy Colombians and using drug trafficking to fund operations. In addition, ELN operatives extort money from multinational and domestic oil companies. In a message posted on "Radio Informaremos," a blog focused on news about social movements, human rights, the environment, and rural matters, the ELN wrote a message about the alleged psychological warfare conducted against the people of Colombia by the U.S. government in conjunction with the Colombian government. The ELN message concluded with:

> Facing this blatant psychological warfare, the revolutionaries and patriots must organize a true communication strategy directed at the public that will allow for the voices of those that have none to be heard, and that will properly represent the true congruence between the people, their social and political forces, and the insurgency in order to defeat any foreign influence upon us.

The ELN's Web site features news, political cartoons, offers for their publications, ELN history, and a frequently-asked-questions section. It appears to be updated on a regular basis, with up-to-date news commentary. A cartoon featured on the main page and also available through YouTube has as its theme, "Colombia: A Country in the Clouds" and criticizes mainstream media's depiction of current events in Colombia.[70]

The network

Extremist Web sites frequently provide links to one another, partly to convey a sense of common participation in a worldwide struggle. The site used by the Indonesian group Laskar Jihad, for example, has featured links to jihadist sites related to Palestine, Afghanistan, Chechnya, and elsewhere. As Merlyna Lim has noted, the images on radical Islamic sites "are a very powerful generator of grievances and religious solidarity—especially among those who are 'far away' from the geographic origin of the conflict depicted."[71]

The number of organizations with Web production capabilities keeps growing, especially in Central Asia. Among these media groups are the following:[72]

- Jundullah Media: an arm of the Islamic Movement of Uzbekistan; in 2009 it released a video featuring German-speaking militants in Afghanistan.
- Ummat Studios: based in Pakistan; produces videos showcasing Taliban operations in Afghanistan and Pakistan.
- Islam Awazi Information Center: a wing of the Turkestan Islamic Party, a largely Uighur group that has claimed credit for attacks in China.

Productions by these and similar groups are usually easily found on the Internet. Their technical quality varies, but the video of many of the combat operations, suicide bomber attacks, and such is often striking. Through the Internet, these groups can reach the world and magnify their importance.

For most extremist organizations around the world, connections with Al Qaeda are limited to an admiring philosophical agreement. Al Qaeda is the paradigm, the group that bloodied the American giant and then defiantly survived a decade of retributive attacks. It is a source of inspiration if not a controlling force within the larger world of terrorism.

In the use of new media, Al Qaeda's prominence is not quite so high. Its As Sahab production company may still be the state-of-the-art exemplar for creating terrorist videos, but it was Al Qaeda in Iraq, the largely autonomous offshoot led by Abu Musab al-Zarqawi, that truly pioneered comprehensive use of the Internet to advance organizational goals. His use of an online press secretary and almost daily online product enhanced his standing among his peers and helped attract attention from the world's news organizations.

Those goals as pursued by Zarqawi exist on several levels, one of which might be called administrative: recruiting, training, providing leadership, and otherwise maintaining as much cohesion as this line of work allows. Another level is, quite simply, to generate terror, by showing the world the viciousness of executions and willingness to die in suicide bombings. Terrorism is far from new, but during recent years Al Qaeda-inspired terrorism has moved into global prominence, aided immeasurably by new media.

3   Terrorists' online strategies

While terrorism is by no means a new phenomenon, the post-9/11 world has greatly focused its efforts on understanding the post-9/11 Muslim world. With images of Arabs in Palestine and Lebanon allegedly celebrating the death of Americans shortly after the attacks, U.S. officials raised the misguided question, "Why do they hate us?" There are many reasons that motivate groups of people to engage in acts of terrorism, but hate is not one of them.

One cannot overestimate the wealth of information available online that can help us better understand the rationale of extremist groups. Thanks to the Internet, we do not need to travel thousands of miles to learn what extremists are thinking, how they view world events, and most importantly, how they justify their actions, including terrorism. Terrorists have a presence online. They are visible, and a study of their extensive network proves that they have created a virtual Habermasian public sphere and they are here to stay. While many citizens around the world oppose U.S. foreign policies, as was evident during the Bush administration's unilateral approach to the Iraq war, only a handful express their frustrations using extreme measures such as terrorism and bringing harm to others. Extremists know they can grab the world's attention with such unconventional methods of violence.

Post 9/11, the lines between who is an Arab, who is a Muslim, and who is a terrorist, were all blurred, and journalism often linked the three categories together in the public's mind. Cases of what appeared to be discrimination against Arabs surfaced across America. Within the first nine weeks after 9/11, the American-Arab Anti-Discrimination Committee reported 700 cases of violent discrimination against Arab-looking people in the United States, including several murders.[1] Discrimination continues today, and can affect Arabs or Muslims, or those thought to be Arabs or Muslims, in all facets of life. Such is the case of an Arab family that was removed from an AirTran flight in January, 2009, because of a misunderstanding resulting from a conversation they were having about the safest place to sit on an airplane.[2] There is reason for hope, nevertheless. A 2009 Pew survey reported that a plurality of Americans (58 percent and 45 percent respectively) agree that Muslims face a lot of discrimination and that "Islam is no more likely than other faiths to encourage violence among its believers."[3]

Extremism is very much alive today, and those who endorse the Huntington *Clash of Civilizations* school of thought believe it is here to stay. Of the 45 organizations designated by the State Department's Office of the Coordinator for Counterterrorism[4] as foreign terrorist organizations in January 2010, eight maintain an online presence. Some are active on one Web site yet most have multiple sites that reinforce their presence. Likeminded organizations provide hyperlinks to each other, creating a network of organizations that is much stronger than its individual members. This creates an active online presence of extremist organizations from different religions, including but not limited to an extremist version of Islam.

Terrorism and the Internet

Schmid and de Graaf noted accurately over two decades ago that communication is at the heart of terrorism.[5] Since the 1990s, Internet use by terrorist groups has been documented[6] and has been referred to as "cyber sanctuary."[7] Terrorists pose two distinct potential threats online: cyberterrorism and the use of the Internet as a communication medium.

Cyberterrorism is the use of the Internet destructively and directly to bring about harm to persons or property, including attacks on Web sites. Cyberterrorism can do this by introducing a virus, altering information online, crashing a Web site, and by inserting a political message in a site belonging to another, among other methods. This is a specific use of the Internet as a communication medium to transmit an attack. Hackers belonging to pro-Israeli, pro-Palestinian, anti-terrorist, and pro-Al Qaeda groups have each played a role in attacking, hacking, or destroying Web sites. Pro-Palestinian attacks have typically targeted commercial and political Israeli Web sites.[8]

Terrorist groups also use the Internet as a communication medium. This is sometimes referred to as the "Dark Web." While definitions of what constitutes a terrorist Web site are not absolute, the number of terrorist Web sites was estimated at a dozen in 1997, 4,350 by early 2005,[9] 4,800 by 2006,[10] and over 6,000 by 2008.[11] Today, most terrorist groups are believed to be online.[12] Al Qaeda was the leader in using the Internet to its advantage: "From the start its leadership seems to have intuitively grasped this enormous communicative potential of the Internet and sought to harness this power both to further the movement's strategic aims and facilitate its tactical operations."[13]

The Internet as a communication medium

Even though current literature and conventional wisdom indicate that Al Qaeda is the number one terrorist threat, this study reveals that a number of organizations, not all of which are affiliated with Al Qaeda, have built a significant presence online but are often ignored by the policymaking, journalistic, and scholarly communities. To better understand their presence, and based on Holsti's (1969) six basic elements of the communication process for content analysis,[14] the following text is divided into six sections:

1 Who is the source of the message?
2 What is the message?
3 Who are the audiences?
4 How and through what channels is the message communicated?
5 What is the purpose of the message?
6 What is the effect of the message?

Who is the source of the message?

Most serious terrorist organizations have an online presence today. Organizations affiliated with a religion usually display verses of their sacred scripture and icons symbolizing their faith, or mention their divine power, be it Allah or another deity. Those associated with a particular country prominently display the flag, a map, or pictures of significant historical sites. Iraqi, Palestinian, Lebanese, Saudi, and Egyptian terrorist organizations all maintain Web sites.

Technologically advanced sites provide "Links to other sites" which conveniently allow users to find like-minded organizations. Al-Muslmeen Army in Iraq provides 17 links to other organizations, although not all the links are functioning, which is not atypical for some of these sites. Once a core list of Web sites is identified, the level of interconnectedness between like-minded organizations is quickly revealed. Al-Boraq Media Organization is responsible for maintaining a number of terrorist sites which connect back to Al-Boraq. Likewise, Hanein Network, a forum available for extremists to discuss their ideas, shares links with numerous insurgency groups.

What is the message?

Organizations use the Internet to share their history and origin with their audiences. A good number of organizations active today grew as resistance movements to foreign occupation and perceived injustices. Some of the organizations resisting the Israeli occupation originated in the 1960s. Some organizations resisting American occupation were launched at the start of the Iraq war in 2003. The mission of Iraqi organizations has been to get rid of foreign occupation by the United States and its allies. Palestinian and Lebanese organizations state their mission as getting rid of the Israeli occupation and liberating Palestine. Most Muslim organizations' sites include heavily religious rhetoric that mentions jihad and the need to spread the teachings of Islam. Mission statements are usually a minimum of one-page long. For the Arabic sites, this is a reflection of the Arabic language and the indirect approach of the Arabic culture often cited by scholars of intercultural communication.

Islamic organizations' doctrines are usually a hybrid of religion and politics. These sites rely heavily on their own interpretation of Islam to guide their actions. Their interpretation of Islam dictates their politics and separating the two is impossible. Non-religious organizations' doctrines are political. Foreign occupation is used as a justification for violent actions. Some organizations' justification is not as explicit, where jihad, spreading Islam, and fighting the enemies of God are all cited as reasons for their advocating violence. Some political beliefs are presented using caricatures. The Jihad and Change Front caricatures, which are available in both Arabic and English, make political statements about the U.S. forces in Iraq. A cartoon on the Jihad and Change Front's Web site depicts two American soldiers standing over an Iraqi body and conversing: "Hey look!!! This body is full of holes, but not made by bullets!!!" says one soldier while the other replies: "They were made from electric drille! Just like we made in Vietnam and El Salvador, we're training death squads, in order to do the dirty war [*sic.*] for us, then we can get back home with our hands clean. He! He! He! He!"

Dates mentioned on the sites include the establishment of the organization, a war anniversary, or a date marking a significant operation for the movement. On the Web site of The Voice of Jihad, information about Paul Marshall, the hostage from Lockheed Martin, and his beheading on June 18, 2004 is available. Some organizations provide information about their leaders and others, such as the Islamic Army in Iraq, include a spokesperson. In a country with less than 1 percent Internet connectivity rate, one can safely assume that the messages are intended to reach outside publics.

Evident from their online banners and seals, these organizations are either patriotic or religious, and advocate resistance to the occupation through armed force. Banners of movements with a military base usually display a weapon or an image of a soldier. Most organizations also have a slogan. Those include religious verses, sometimes from sacred scriptures. The Jihad and Reform Front's slogan reads: "And hold fast, all of you together, to the Rope of Allah (i.e., the Qur'an), and be not devided amoung [*sic.*] yourselves." Other slogans are nonreligious and reference the occupation and the need for the followers to unite.

Martyrs are an important aspect of a terrorist organization's identity. In some cases, sites dedicate a full section to martyrs. Ezzedeen Al-Qassam Brigades' site contains an elaborate section including the name of the martyr, his/her picture, and the date of the operation. The user can click on the martyr's picture to read a brief biography, a press release about the operation and the martyr, see additional photos of the martyr, and watch a video of the martyr reading his/her will while reciting a few verses from the Qur'an. Both pictures and videos usually show the martyr in uniform holding a rifle. The Popular Front for the Liberation of Palestine's site also provides an elaborate section for its martyrs, although these martyrs are not necessarily insurgents killed during an operation. According to the site, most members are said to have been killed by Israeli attacks. The Popular Front's database has a search function that allows users to search using the name of the martyr or the date of the operation (although the search by date function does not work). The database contains 382 members dating back to 1968, the year the organiza-tion was established. The most recent martyr listed died in November, 2008. Some sites do not mention the martyrs by name. The Baghdad Sniper's site refers to all its martyrs as Baghdad Snipers. The Islamic Army in Iraq refers to its martyrs as such without using their actual names. Showcasing the martyrs seems to be an important online tool that these organizations use to stress the importance of armed resistance and of sacrificing oneself. For the Muslim organizations, the martyrs' farewell videos borrow heavily from the Qur'an to legitimize their actions.

Additionally, sites such as that of Ezzedeen Al-Qassam Brigades have sec-tions dedicated to prisoners. The Al-Aqsa Martyrs Brigade site devotes a section to the Palestinian prisoners in Israeli jails. The Popular Front for the Liberation of Palestine's site contains a section on prisoners' affairs with recent updated information about their situation, and the Popular Front for the Liberation of Palestine–General Command has a section on memoirs of prisoners detailing their life story. By showcasing prisoners, the organization shows its concern for their members and their wellbeing.

Martyrdom lends itself to a discussion about the place of jihad in Islam. After 9/11, Islam came under increased scrutiny in non-Muslim countries that did not know much about the religion. Like Judaism, Islam is both a religion and a way of life. Thus, it is important to understand the place of jihad in Islam, since references to the connection with Islam are included in many of the Muslim Web sites.

"Jihad is the name of all effort, exertion, and endurance that each Muslim demonstrates in order to be bestowed with the pleasure of God."[15] In the Arabic language, jihad means exertion of effort. A close study of Islam reveals that it is a religion of peace,[16] and M. Futhullah Gülen noted that terror has no place in real Islam.[17] There are rules concerning conduct in times of war, and all of these rules require treating the enemy with respect and not targeting civilians. Islam outlaws the use of terror.[18] As highlighted by Bulaç, the meaning of jihad has been hijacked by extremists from its ori-ginal meaning of removing obstacles that stand between oneself and the worship of God, to its new meaning involving the use of terror by extreme Islamists in the name of religion.[19]

Equally important is a brief discussion about suicide attacks. There is no agreement in the scholarly community about what constitutes a suicide attack and whether it should be labeled suicide terrorism, which ascribes a negative value to the act.[20] Japanese Kamikaze suicide pilots acting on behalf of their state against the Allied forces during World War II may be considered terrorists, although one could argue that any act directed at combatant enemies is not terrorism. Formulated by Ayman al-Zawahiri and Osama bin Laden, the notion of global jihad by Muslims was put to test in the early 1990s.[21] In the case of suicide missions on behalf of Islam, the perpetrators of the attacks label them-selves as martyrs since suicide is forbidden by the religion. Thus the conduct of suicide attacks by extremist Muslims is referred to as martyrdom.[22]

Organizations also pinpoint their enemies online. Enemies could be a country such as the United States, Israel, or a general category of people, the infidels. While the United States could be listed as an enemy, this does not stop the organization from referencing U.S. studies to support their claims. Al-Shahid Foundation quotes a study done by Harvard confirming that orphaned children who grow up in homes with families perform better academically by the age of four than children who are raised at orphanages. The study was also reported by Al Jazeera. Politically aligned organizations are referred to as "friends." Web links to other organizations are an indication of friendship.

Al-Muslmeen Army in Iraq divides its operations into four sections: attacks, destruction, rockets, and sniper operations. Most of those organizations provide press releases, sharing their news with the site users and media outlets. The Jihad on the Land of Rafedean Brigades–News Network site has a link to its own TV station and posts radio news clips. In addition to their followers, these releases target media outlets. These organizations report news based on their own interpretation and political analysis as opposed to the way the news was reported by mainstream media.

In addition to sharing their news with the world, some sites such as *PFLF-GC*, report world news and news from "enemy'" media outlets, listed as Israeli. Some sites go as far as monitoring news coverage about their organization as well as sharing media appearances. The site of Al-Shahid Foundation provides a section titled "The Foundation in the News" that monitors relevant articles. The Baghdad Sniper site lists articles about its organization in Chinese, Spanish, and Italian media outlets, both print and video. The PFLF-GC's site lists an article about an interview conducted by a Russian TV station with their General Director. The Islamic Front for the Iraqi Resistance site has a section monitoring the organization in the news. The Islamic Resistance Movement's site has an article on an NBC interview conducted with counter-terrorism expert Evan Kohlmann. This active monitoring implies that the organizations are well aware of creating what Hoffman referred to as "Internet buzz," hoping that their news will end up in mainstream media.[23]

Not only can one access current press releases, but some sites conveniently provide archives. *Al-Fateh Magazine*, which is the Hamas children's magazine, archives its issues online.

While some literature on terrorism identifies fundraising as one of the main purposes of terrorist sites,[24] the authors came across few sites that mention the possibility of donating funds. The Brigades of the Martyr Ezzedeen Al-Qassam site has an email address with the word "fund" in the username: fund@alqassam.ps. Sites do, however, ask for support in spreading the organization's message.

In conclusion, these organizations are presenting themselves as religious and patriotic armed resistance movements and are accordingly sharing their missions and previous operations with their audiences. Evident from the press monitors and the documents provided, the organizations are concerned about their image outside of the country of operation, as any good public relations professional would be. In an attempt to legitimize the organization, many provide research, publications, and books. While most of the research is by regional scholars, Western studies are quoted on occasion to support their arguments. The existence of archives and research materials may be used to present the organization as more scholarly and legitimate. The PFLF-GC provides a book reviews section. The Islamic Resistance Movement includes an Islamic Library. Jamaat Ansar Al-Sunna's site library contains over 80 religious documents and books. Al-Mojahideen has a link to books in English about different types of weapons.

To whom

The language of a site is an indicator of the intended message target. Terrorist Web sites are available in a multitude of languages, which is a clear indication that the organizations are targeting audiences beyond their host nation's language.

Often sites are either translated into another language or provide the user with the option to access Google Translate, a free function that translates text automatically. Some sites only offer a small section of their online text in a different language. The Nationalist and Islamic Front's site has a section dedicated to English articles, while Al-Shahid Foundation's mission is translated into English. The Islamic Army in Iraq's site encourages its users to submit their own translations:

> Official English website's administration recommend the army Ideology translation. If you have the capability of translating one of these two statements, translate them and send the here to the website administration in order to publish them officially after checking the translation.

The Baghdad Sniper's site is available in nine languages: Arabic, English, Spanish, French, Turkish, Urdu, German, Italian, and Chinese. The numerous spelling and grammar mistakes imply that the translators are not native speakers.

The overwhelming majority of terrorist Web sites are geared toward men who are encouraged to join the movement. Nevertheless, some sites are directed to women (see Chapter 5). This is an indication that the generally patriarchal groups that Reinares[25] and Russell and Miller[26] referred to may be changing. Nonetheless, males continue to dominate online. *Tawhid and Jihad Forum's* drop-down list includes the names of 140 authors, all of whom are male. There are a few exceptions, however. One occurred on the Army of Saad bin Abi Waqas site, which features a female author named Um Omar Al-Farooq, the mother of Omar Al-Farooq. Other sites target the young, such as *Al Fateh Magazine*.

In addition to targeting men, women, and children, the presence of press releases indicates that the organizations are reaching out to media outlets directly. As Dallal argues in the case of Hizballah, the organization counters and challenges mainstream depictions of its resistance movements.[27] Similarly, Eedle and Ali refer to terrorist videos as a "21st Century media war."[28] The organizations are clearly targeting audiences beyond their state borders by offering their Web sites in multiple languages. The sites also reveal that the traditional adult male-dominant sites are slightly changing, with an increased role for women and children.

How

This section examines the functionality of the site and its multimedia features, the establishment of a virtual community, and the available communication options.

Today, only a small portion of the sites are text only; most have multimedia applications and user-friendly features. Search functions allow the users to navigate the site, with some including a drop-down list of sections from which the user could choose. Pictures, audios and videos offer additional elements, especially to younger audiences. Most sites have an indication of when they were last updated. This ranges from a daily update to a couple of months. The majority, however, are updated on a regular basis.

Pictures depict the organization, the people of the country of operation, or the country itself. Most of the pictures are of the organization, showcasing military power and martyrs who are usually dressed in army uniforms posing with a rifle and a Qur'an in what appears to be the last few hours prior to their assigned operation. Many pictures are of martyrs in action during an operation. Some are of the organization's prisoners and their leaders. Ansar Al-Sunna's photos include an album with pictures of its members giving away meat during Eid (a Muslim religious holiday). Some pictures showcase the military power of the group and their soldiers in training. The second category of pictures focuses on the suffering of the population. This shows the pictures of the dead and the wounded, sometimes children. The purpose is to highlight the aggression and destruction caused by the enemy. Finally, the third category shows landscapes of the country. Very few sites have a slideshow.

Audio files contain numerous patriotic and military songs, Qur'an chanting, and lectures by prominent figures, many of them religious. Among the PLF's songs are those titled "Following your Footsteps Abu Abbas" and "Place the Flag Higher." The Al-Nasser Salah Addin's Brigade's Web site includes songs titled "The Hero's Blood," "Strike your Enemy," and "Lucky Martyr." Some audio files are of men chanting Qur'an verses. Others contain lectures by prominent religious or political figures. These lectures serve the purpose of educating, motivating, and inspiring. The Army Men of Al-Nakshabandia Way's site has mobile ringtones based on their songs.

Insurgents' videos posted online continue to be a favorite method of reaching their audiences. Realizing the importance of propaganda and the media war with the United States, Muslim groups started producing jihadi videos as early as the 1980s.[29] With the start of Al Qaeda in the 1990s, the growth of the Internet, and the launch of the war in Iraq, these videos gained momentum. Some sites have fewer than 10 videos and others go as high as 500. *The Islamic Front for the Iraqi Resistance* has 546 filmed operations and the user has the option to report broken links, a function not available on most sites. Eedle and Ali describe these videos as the "21st Century media war."

Different types of videos are produced, all of which showcase the organization in a victorious light. These include ideological lectures in which authoritative Muslim sources share their philosophy and worldviews. Others contain interviews with high-level figures from the organization. Some videos are informational and include talks and lectures on jihad. According to Eedle and Ali, propaganda documentaries usually decry the hypocrisy of the U.S. freedom and democracy slogans and its actions which include the support of Israel and the killing of thousands of Iraqis. Some videos celebrate big operations and brag about small gains. Some showcase martyrs in their last appearance before their operation. *The Army Men of Al-Nakshabandia Way* has links to mobile footage for videotaped operations. The videos particularly glorify martyrdom. On IAI's site, all of the videos showcase the organization winning against the United States and its allies. An example is a 19-minute video on IAI's site that shows martyrs in action as they are killed. There is also background information about the martyrs, the operation in which they were engaged, and the ceremonies that honored them. The videos have IAI's banner and seal and are accompanied by religious songs and by Qur'an chanting. Soundtracks are very common in all videos.

Some video operations incorporate gruesome images. The most notorious videos show terrorists beheading civilians. Nicholas Berg's beheading by the Jordanian al-Zarqawi in 2004 gained world recognition. Other videos glorify jihadi heroes and martyrs, showing their metaphoric ascendance to heaven. Standard editing software including Windows Movie Maker is used to produce these videos. Editors usually mix their own footage with mainstream news footage to convey their message. The main purpose of these videos is to counter the traditional media depiction of wars,[30] whether these depictions are sympathetic or not to the terrorists' message. By producing alternative news bulletins, these organizations share their uncensored view of the world in the hope of inspiring recruits. By using extreme violence, the videos shock their audiences.

News organizations in the region register to download jihadi videos, and in return the sites proudly display the media logos. Nevertheless, these videos are still filtered to create a specific message that is supportive of jihad. For example, The Mahdi Army only show their operations against the far enemy, the United States, but not against other Iraqi groups.[31] Such videos are not produced in the Middle East only. For example, some young Muslims in Britain are making their own creative videos.

While the dangers posed by these videos are debatable, jihadi videos on the Internet remain an important source of information and a virtual tie to the organization for radicals and recent converts. The videos may also lure new recruits eager to join the movement.[32] Kohlmann refers to a 2004 case in Italy where police eavesdropped on a recruiter playing a video to a future suicide bomber and noted the positive reaction of the follower.

In addition to videos, a few sites have flash clips featuring animated movies. Al-Jamaa Al-Islamiya has 8 religious flash clips in Arabic. Each clip is less than 10 minutes long. One titled *You* [female] *Who Want to be Saved* is narrated by a man addressing a woman who stopped fasting and praying, who was now going out with men and seducing them, and taking inappropriate pictures of herself without the veil and posting them on the Internet. The narrator asks the woman if she is afraid of God and if she wants to be saved. The end of the clip shows the woman wearing the veil (the viewer cannot see her face) walking on the road to heaven. In another flash clip entitled *The Nation of Mohammad*, a man calls on the nation of Prophet Mohammad to defend the Prophet who has been insulted by the Infidels and to "harshly" fight the infidels.

Multimedia files educate users about issues relevant to the movement, as well as motivate and inspire the audience to act by joining the movement and spreading its mission. Some sites allow its users to download different quality levels of the same file depending on the user's connection speed, making the site more user-friendly. The user has the option to watch the videos in what is labeled as "great quality," "good quality," or "mobile quality." The use of multimedia files indicates a level of technical sophistication and offers an entertaining alternative to simple text. The presence of mobile ringtones on a few sites is evidence of the organization reaching out to younger audiences. The presence of mobile video footage on some sites indicates that a younger generation is probably involved in the movement.

In terms of functionality, most of the sites have format errors. These include broken links or missing files. This is especially true for the multimedia links. In some cases, over 30 video links are available for the same video. For example, for each audio and video clip, there are usually numerous multimedia links available. Since the links are often shut down, the organization offers more than one link as a back-up plan. Most sites offered in English or that include English text have spelling and grammar errors. Al-Rashedeen's Arabic site has a video titled "Bells of Dangerous [*sic.*]" instead of "Bells of Danger." On average, a typical site with less than 100 links has 95 percent of its links functioning. This number ranges, though, from zero, such as The Voice of Jihad's site, to 100 percent functioning links.

Other user-friendly functions include listserves and RSS features which allow the organization to maintain a steady line of communication with its publics. A few sites allow users to e-mail an article or share the site with a friend: *Jihad and Tawhid Forum*, *PFLF-GC*, and Al-Jamaa Al-Islamiya. Al-Jamaa Al-Islamiya's site also has other Web 2.0 features including a section for Islamic e-cards. Users can personalize the card by including a message and then send it to a friend. The categories for the cards are God's names, Ramadan greetings, special occasions and birthdays, religious phrases, pictures of God's creation (pictures from nature), and other scenic pictures. When the user registers, he/she can get a personal e-mail address with the organization's domain name. The Islamic Resistance Movement supplies the option of adding its site to "favorites."

Poster competitions are popular on a number of sites. Users are encouraged to design posters that depict the organization and its work, usually with the organization's seal embedded. Some include an icon from the country such as a map, the American flag, either burning or torn, the group's military in action, men, women, and children carrying weapons, and so forth. The designs are creative and all depict the organization as powerful and invincible. IAI's poster competition is titled "Jihad and Good Competition." Six posters are displayed by individual users and another 17 by *Al Zalzalah Jihadist Campaign*. While IAI labeled its competition as such, a number of sites encourage their users to submit posters that represent the organization, usually with the organization's seal included. The Islamic Resistance in Lebanon did not include games in its Web site but did reference a videogame called *Special Force 2—The Story of the True Promise* (*Hikayat al-wa'd Al-Sadek*) which details the life of a martyr. Al-Jamaa Al-Islamiya has a contest during Ramadan which consists of religious questions. The first winner, a female, received an award of approximately US$70 (400 Egyptian Jineih). *Al-Fateh Magazine*, which is the children's site, includes five simple children's games. One asks the user to find the shadow in the picture. The shadow appears to be that of an Israeli soldier. Posters and games are not the only ways used to keep the users engaged. Ansar al-Islam's site provides an example of involving the users, announcing on its site that it will soon be featuring their "best member, best supervisor, best section, and best topic."

As for communication options, most sites have an online feedback form which requires users to enter their name, the subject of the message, the message, and an attachment. Some forms also have a security feature that requires users to enter a distorted series of characters and numbers for verification purposes. Some sites, such as *Tawhid and Jihad Forum*, have a disclaimer that the organization does not necessarily share the views of the authors. A few provide an e-mail address, phone or fax number, and a mailing address. A number of sites have links to magazines and newsletters, with some having guest books. All of these communication options allow users to maintain contact with and contribute comments to these organizations. The IAI site publishes *Al-Fursan* (The Knights) *Magazine* which is issued on a regular basis. The latest issue covered topics on gathering intelligence in the era of globalization, lessons from the battlefield, education in the faith, and continuing the success of the jihadist media. The *Tawhid and Jihad Forum* links to two magazines: *Al-Ansar Magazine* and *The Group Magazine*. *Baghdad Sniper* has a link to a newsletter although the link is broken. *PFLF-GC* has a magazine entitled *Ila Al Amam* (Moving Forward) *Until the Land and People are Liberated*. The Army Men of Al-Nakshabandia Way's site has a magazine entitled *The Magazine of the Army*. The Islamic Front for the Iraqi Resistance's magazine is *Al-Jame' Magazine* (i.e. *The Mosque Magazine*). The Islamic Resistance Movement's magazine is *Pioneers of Excellency*. Abu Ali Mustafa Brigades' magazine is *The Revolution is Ongoing*. Al-Mojahideen's magazine is entitled *The Voice of Jihad* (*Sawt Al-Jihad*). It provides 29 editions, but none of the links are functioning. There are also links to 22 editions of *Al-Battar Camp Bulletin*, all of which are broken.

Forums and comments allow users to share their opinions with the organization. Other types of user-generated content include providing translations for the Web sites. Al-Aqsa Martyrs Brigade's site allows users to post hyperlinks and videos; videos can also be rated. Some sites allow users to contribute content, although it is not always clear if the content on a given site has been produced by users or by contributing authors. Some sites allow users to share hyperlinks. Guest books are also a popular way to allow users to share their impressions of the organization.

All these features that allow users to stay connected with the organization and interact with other members help create what Eedle and Ali[33] and Thomas[34] have referred to as virtual community. Eedle and Ali observe that videos and the Internet allow the organization to maintain a virtual tie with its supporters. Thomas notes that the Internet creates solidarity and a platform for members to build and maintain a physical base. Sagemen has argued that passive Web sites only reinforce users' current beliefs, but that interactivity features could potentially recruit individuals.[35] While there are a range of Web 2.0 features on many of these sites, and while users are able to voice their opinions, censorship and forum rules continue to restrict what can be written. The organizations allow like-minded individuals to share their comments, but dissent is not usually tolerated.

Why

Traditionally, scholars have argued that terrorists use the Internet as a communication medium to serve the following purposes: disseminate propaganda,[36] organize people,[37] communicate information,[38] fundraise,[39] and recruit.[40] Other uses that have received less attention from the scholarly community, yet are equally significant, are countering mainstream media and educating the public about the organization and its cause. The distinction between propaganda and information is not always carefully drawn in these uses. Steinfatt defines propaganda as "a form of persuasion involving mass message campaign designed to discourage thought and to suppress evidence."[41] There is plenty of room to debate whether or not terrorist sites publishing military gains are communicating information or disseminating propaganda.

The uses of the Internet to organize and communicate greatly overlap. Many incidents in the past 10 years speak to the use of computers and the Internet by terrorist groups to organize and communicate. In the recent 2008 Mumbai attacks, terrorists relied on Voice Over Internet Protocol (VOIP) to connect to one another.[42] The October 2005 attacks in Bali are another example of terrorists relying on computers to plan their attack.[43] The planning document, which was found on one of the terrorists' computers, was called "The Bali Project." The Internet is also likely to have played a role in the 2005 London bombings.[44] The slaying of Daniel Pearl in 2002 was announced via an e-mail message sent to news outlets.[45] Similarly, the planning of the 9/11 attacks was facilitated by the use of the Internet.[46] Investigators found encrypted messages in password-protected areas of a Web site that were sent using public emails, for example Hotmail or Yahoo, via the Internet in public places such as libraries or Internet cafes. The use of Pretty Good Privacy (PGP—a computer application used to send e-mail messages with increased security), however, is not uncommon in sending e-mail messages. Shortly after 9/11 and the U.S. attacks on Afghanistan, activity online confirmed that Al Qaeda used the Internet to regroup.[47]

In addition to communicating for the purposes of orchestrating an event, the Internet is also used by terrorists to communicate with the public. In late 2007, As Sahab, which is Al Qaeda's media arm, took questions from the public to which al-Zawahiri responded.[48] According to the report, comments posted included people seeking advice, offering criticism, and calling for more action by the group. As Thomas notes, the Internet creates solidarity among members of the same group, replacing a physical base with a virtual one.[49]

Terrorists use the Internet for financial support, either by fundraising through the traditional means of asking sympathizers to donate money, or by engaging in cyberfraud, including soliciting personal information from victims through scam e-mails.[50] U.S. Federal investigators' efforts to catch such criminals have been described as "an escalating game of digital cat-and-mouse with cyberterrorists."[51]

Because terrorists can use the Internet to fully control the content of their message without relying entirely on mainstream media, the Internet facilitates recruiting.[52] Messages can be tailored to specific audiences, and in their own languages.

In summary, the purpose of all the sites appears to be informing their audiences, communicating with them, and persuading them to change their opinion about the organization. Some sites make heavy mention of martyrdom and glorify it. *The Voice of Jihad* served the purpose of communicating hostage terms. A small number of sites fundraise online. A recurring theme in many of the sites, however, is justification. Most seem to be fully aware of their unfavorable depiction in mainstream media. They use their online presence to counter these depictions and to justify their values and actions to skeptics. On the PFLP's site, an article titled "Campaign to Remove 'Terrorist' Designations" argued that the designation of the PFLP and other Palestinian organizations as terrorist groups is yet another attempt by the United States to criminalize popular resistance movements and intimidate the Palestinians. In another article posted on the Web site of The Islamic Resistance [*sic*.] Movement titled "The Resistance, the Occupation, and the War of

Terms," the author wrote about the occupiers' advantage in framing issues in the media. The article referenced scholars' difficulty in agreeing on a definition for terrorism. Likewise the author spoke of the enemies' misuse of words such as extremism and terrorism, as well as martyrs and suicide bombers. Based on the sheer number of languages these sites are available in, it is reasonable to assume that the organizations are targeting international audiences. Although almost all the sites offered a way to communicate with the organization, be it an online form or an e-mail address, most do not offer explicit directions on how to join the movement.

With what effect

There are two indicators of the effects of these sites and their data on the users. The first indicator is the forums and discussions sections of the sites that have them. These usually have explicit regulations for their users about the terms of conduct. Each forum has an administrator with the right to delete posts for any reason. They ask users to refrain from choosing inappropriate user names. They also prohibit members from using insults and words that hurt, and from promoting services. Some forums keep track of how many times a user has broken forum rules. *Ezzedeen Al-Qassam Brigades*'s users have a maximum of five fines before their user account is blocked by the administrator. The user's rule-breaking record appears on his/her profile and can be viewed by other users.

The lack of a democratic atmosphere may discourage members who have not yet been radicalized from participating in the groups' activities. On *Al-Aqsa Martyrs Brigade*'s forum, one of the users posted a comment asking users to engage in a real debate. His post was followed by a few other posts that agreed and stressed the importance of members expressing their opinion in the forum. The final post was from a user who did not agree with the importance of freedom of speech. This user warned of the critical comments that some members could post and argued that the organization would not tolerate any insulting comments. On *Ezzedeen Al-Qassam Brigades*'s forum there was a discussion thread titled "Who is Bin Laden? Know your leaders, Muslims." The post bragged about bin Laden and glorified his achievements, presenting him as a leader of Muslims. A post replying to that post complained that unfavorable opinions about bin Laden should not be deleted. Some forums keep track of their users' countries. *PFLP-GC* allegedly has members from 80 countries including members from 39 American states.

The second indicator is the polls which some sites use to query users about political and social issues in the region. When *The Islamic Front for the Iraqi Resistance* asked about President Obama's policy in Iraq and whether it differed from that of President Bush. The four possible answers were "no," "somewhat," "yes," and "I don't know." Of the 392 votes cast, 41 percent voted "yes", 30 percent voted "somewhat", 25 percent voted "no", and 4 percent voted "I don't know" as of April 13, 2009. This is a small indication of what users of the sites are thinking and their more favorable opinion of President Obama as compared to President Bush. However, it is worth noting that some polls use procedures that may create problems in the interpretation of the results. *Al-Nasser Salah Addin's Brigade*'s poll asked about "the fate of the Cairo Dialogue between the factions." A few asked about international politics. *The Jihad and Change Front*'s poll asked: "What do you expect to happen after the withdrawal of the occupying forces in Iraq?" The four options and votes were as follows: 67 percent voted "Empowerment to the Jihadi project," 25 percent "domestic fights," 4 percent "dividing Iraq," and 4 percent "continuing the current political situation." The number of votes cast was unknown on April 13, 2009.

Language differences

When sites are translated, they usually present a shorter version of the text, and the translated site lacks the technical sophistication of its counterpart in the native language. Translated sites are also often plagued with spelling and grammatical mistakes to varying degrees. On Hezbollah's site, and according to the visitor numbers presented by the organization, fewer people visited the English version as compared to the Arabic one. Those visiting the English site were more critical of the organization as reflected by the polls available on the site.

Summary

Today, terrorist Web sites include numerous user-friendly features and applications. Users have the option to download files, join discussion boards and chat rooms, learn about the gains of the insurgencies, e-mail articles to friends, contact the media department of the organization, and train to be insurgents using posted videos. In comparison to U.S. government agencies' Web sites, researchers found that "terrorist/extremist groups adopted similar levels of Web technologies ... [and] significantly more sophisticated multimedia technologies."[53]

Terrorist Web sites aim to reach potential sympathizers and future recruits. By disseminating information regarding their mission and beliefs, and by establishing a theological rationale for their actions, organizations are seeking prospective members. Some sites even offer items for sale, including T-shirts and videos.[54] One purpose of the Web sites is to establish the organization's presence and to instill fear in the public. In the case of Hizballah, Dallal argues that in addition to recruitable subjects, the organization "also addresses imaginable audiences of nonrecruitable subjects."[55] Depending on the purpose of the organization, the enemy changes. Nevertheless, common enemies include American and Israeli nationals, businessmen, government officials, and tourists.[56] Shaping international public opinion by influencing journalists's work is yet another purpose.[57]

Why use the Internet?

Globalization has clearly played a role in the start and growth of terrorist Web sites. Thanks to technological advancements and the relatively cheap cost of the Internet, terrorist groups are able to utilize this new medium effectively. Weimann suggests that we think of terrorist groups today as transnational and transregional in character, not regional or state-bound.[58] The traditional North-to-South and West-to-East model of information flow is challenged by these groups and the messages they are communicating. Terrorist organizations counter mainstream media depictions of their resistance movements.[59] By offering alternative voices to the public sphere, they hope to alter public opinion and gain support for their cause. The rhetoric used by mainstream media as compared with the terrorist Web sites is significantly different. Mainstream media focus on the violence of the terrorists, but the Web sites of these organizations "try in many ways to appear like the websites of legitimate political organizations."[60] These Web sites may allow terrorist organizations to bypass the media and communicate their messages directly to their audiences, providing a wealth of information about the organization, their mission, and background.

There are many convincing reasons why terrorist groups may use the Internet as a communication medium as an element of their terrorist activities. Because the Internet is a relatively new technology, regulations surrounding its use in many countries are just now being enacted: "as an open, decentralized interoperable network, regulations are few in number and impose minimal constraints."[61] To date, no U.S. statutes directly address the issue of blocking terrorist Web sites or prosecuting the owners or operators. Some sections of the Patriot Act and the Protect America Act are cited to support government actions against Web sites affiliated or linked to terrorism. First, there are statutes that authorize surveillance or monitoring: 18 USC §3123 (2007), 18 USC §2703 (2007), and 50 USC §1805 (2007). Second, there are statutes that make certain actions illegal, such as raising funds for terrorists: 18 USC §1030 (2007), 18 USC §2339A (2007), and 18 USC §2339B (2007). These may serve the basis for government action against a Web site such as blocking it and prosecuting its operator. In recent years, stories about U.S. Internet Service Providers (ISP) unknowingly hosting terrorist Web sites were reported in the U.S. media. Fortune ITX is one of many such companies that hosted sites encouraging attacks on Americans and Israelis.[62] Since there are no criminal ramifications to the launch of a Web site in the United States, terrorist organizations may proceed with spreading their message online using such hosts.

Another reason that terrorists use the Internet is its anonymous nature.[63] Terrorists often use public libraries and free e-mail accounts to communicate electronically. Encrypted messages and steganography (hiding a message, perhaps within an image) are also used. Software programs such as Six/Four and Camera/Shy are used by hackers to ensure anonymity and to secretly store and retrieve information.[64] Most of these employ some form of PGP encryption, and net-savvy terrorists also use unprotected server space to save files. For example, George Washington University and the Arkansas State Highway and Transportation Department discovered jihadi videos on their servers.[65]

In 2002, Microsoft researchers coined the term "darknet" at a conference to refer to the Internet black market.[66] Terrorist Web sites, once shut down, often migrate to a different address, "websites suddenly emerge, frequently modify their formats, and then swiftly disappear—or in many cases, seem to disappear by changing their online address but retaining much the same content."[67] These tactics make the tracking of users by counterterrorism groups very difficult.

As a global communication medium, the Internet has the potential to reach millions of users.[68] Ideas can flow freely across country boundaries, connecting people with similar ideologies and thus expanding the network.[69] This is evident in the number of Web sites being offered in multiple languages. For example, the Web site of the Islamic Army in Iraq is available in Arabic, English, French, and Spanish.[70] Since there are virtually no space limitations, terrorists can post volumes of training materials, thus building an online library.[71] The relatively low cost of the Internet, which obviously varies from one country to another, allows terrorist groups to reach audiences in homes or Internet cafés. Most importantly, the posting of press releases and videos online creates an "Internet buzz" in the hope that the group's news will appear in mainstream media.[72]

How real a threat?

The debate about the full capacity and the threat from terrorists' use of the Internet continues. Multiple factors play a role: globalization, laws and regulations, Internet penetration, and interactivity.

"The contemporary global mediascape is a setting in which anyone with a computer can communicate globally, institutions have less control, and states cannot completely regulate information flows."[73] Some scholars argue that shifts from physical to virtual sanctuaries will bring about a "Net war" and that "network-based conflict and crime will become major phenomena in the decades ahead."[74] Although the terrorists' message has a potentially global reach, the digital divide slows down this process: "limited access in most regions and for most of the population of the world obviously limits the Web's capacity to foster political participation."[75] It is important to remember that as of late 2009, only a quarter of the world's population was connected to the Internet;[76] in other words about 1.7 billion people. Internet penetration rates range from a low of virtually 1 percent in Iraq to a high of 100 percent in the Falkland Islands followed by 93 percent in Iceland. The U.S.A. is the 19th top nation with Internet connectivity of 74 percent. The type of connection—broadband versus dial-up—can also severely limit the utility of these sites, especially those that require a high-speed connection for downloading videos and other multimedia files. Low regional Internet connectivity coupled with the fact that many sites are offered in multiple languages has led researchers to believe that the main purpose of terrorists' Web sites is to spread fear in developed nations where Internet connectivity is high. In addition to the digital divide, accessibility may limit the effectiveness of these sites. Depending on the regulations of each country and any filtering software used by their government, some sites may not be locally accessible.

Kimmage argues that Al Qaeda is stuck in a Web 1.0 world in which information is controlled and transmitted top-down. While the interactive features found on Web 2.0 are not being utilized by many of these groups, Kimmage argues that counterterrorism experts can use these features and sites, such as YouTube, to pursue the war on terrorism.[77] Sageman asserts that passive Web sites only reinforce current beliefs.[78] However, the interactive features of some have the potential to recruit individuals and keep the organization visible. To provide a recent example, when al-Zawahiri asked the public to send questions they would like to ask him online, answers were posted four months later.[79]

Lewis argued that "cyberattacks may not have the dramatic and political effect that meets the psychological needs of terrorists to commit violent acts."[80] Hoffman clarified that there are no conclusive results as to whether online tools are effective in recruiting potential members: "it should be emphasized that U.S. government analysts report there is as yet no direct evidence specifically linking the Internet to recruitment of individuals to mainstream established terrorist organizations or movements."[81] Coll and Glasser[82] and others insist that organizations such as Al Qaeda continue to rely on traditional means of communication in training camps and radical mosques: "informal linkages and shared values ... can only be fostered through personal contact."[83] Moreover, "the Internet empowers small groups and makes them appear much more capable than they might actually be."[84] Thus virtual terror may indeed be a problem, but it may be one that is exaggerated and magnified from its real life size. Nevertheless, as the pervasiveness of new technologies increases, counterterrorism and antiterrorism officials would be foolish not to recognize the potential effects of new-media-oriented terrorist groups.

In terms of videos, Eedle and Ali argue that their impact is relatively minimal. They concluded that young Muslims do not actively seek these videos online.[85] Reality as experienced by some segments of the Middle Eastern population, especially those living under dire circumstances particularly in Iraq, Palestine, Lebanon (and also Afghanistan), is sufficient to contribute to the radicalization process without help from the Internet. Images of Arabs dying in these regions are transmitted via satellite channels like Al Jazeera and Al Arabiya to millions of households in the region on a daily basis. These images may motivate young Arabs to sympathize with acts of terrorism directed at the United States, Britain, and Israel. The videos, of course, help in the process of radicalization. As many argue, "online activities substantially improve the ability of such terrorist groups to raise funds, lure new faithful and reach a mass audience."[86]

4 Targeting the young

If the terrorist population comprised a measurable and static number of people—Osama bin Laden's gang and the like—terrorism could probably be controlled, if not altogether eliminated, through a war of attrition. Members of terrorist groups could be picked off by counterterrorism strikes or they would eventually just fade away.

Terrorist leaders recognize that and so understand that they must emphasize recruiting to meet their long-term as well as short-term needs. They also know, as pragmatists, that young people in their ranks can have unique operational value. They often have no paper trail of travel, arrests, or other personal history that might alert security services to their potential roles in terrorist activity. They can be used for everything from messengers to suicide bombers. Away from the battlefield, Internet-savvy teenagers have been given substantial responsibilities in designing terrorist organizations' online operations.

These young people may be motivated by ingenuous idealism or religious devotion, but they may also be acting out a fantasy of adventure without fully realizing the harm they might do to others and to themselves. Sometimes their poverty and desperate circumstances are taken advantage of by recruiters, and they become the youngest mercenaries. More than 300,000 boys and girls under age 18 are estimated to be serving as combatants in almost 75 percent of the world's conflicts. In 80 percent of these wars, there are child fighters under age 15, and in 18 percent, fighters less than 12 years old. Terrorist organizations are well aware that young people constitute an easy-to-reach, easy-to-recruit supply of personnel.[1]

One appraisal of this situation found that

> terrorist organizations exploit the innocent look of children and teenagers, which does not arouse suspicion and enables them to blend into populated areas. In addition, these children and teenagers, who have not yet reached adulthood, are more susceptible to the terrorist organizations' influence and the recruitment of suicide bombers.[2]

The Ashbal Al Qaeda (Lion Cubs of Al Qaeda) have made their appearance in Morocco, Iraq, and places in between. Videos of the Cubs show the young children running with rifles with a patriotic song playing in the background. One of the children who is interviewed begins by saying, "From a mujahid, the son of a mujahid, to all the Muslims," and he urges other children to join the movement "to fight the Zionists and their allies."[3] In August 2009, three "Ashbals" were arrested in Baghdad along with six of their adult trainers. The children were apparently being paid about US$85 per operation, which involved transporting improvised explosive devices (IEDs) by bicycle and motorbike. One of the children said he had taken part in three IED operations. The adult terrorists like using the children because they are usually not searched and on their bikes they can easily navigate narrow alleyways. At about the same time, Iraqi security forces also announced that they had arrested four children under age 14 in Kirkuk, part of a group calling itself "Birds of Paradise" (an allusion to martyrdom), who had been recruited by adults to conduct suicide bombing attacks.[4]

For the terrorist organizations that enlist these foot soldiers, new media provide invaluable recruiting venues. A quick search for online fare will find videos of mujahideen in action—fighting (successfully) against U.S. troops is always a favorite—with blood-stirring martial music in the background and a subtle or not-so-subtle recruiting message tacked on. Economic conditions among young people in many parts of the world increase their susceptibility to such messages. In many Arab countries and elsewhere, joblessness is especially high, leaving teenagers and young adults idle and willing to take risks to escape a boring, dead-end existence. (According to the World Bank, the unemployment rate for the Middle East and North Africa in 2005—the most recent available data—was 12.1 percent.[5] In some countries and among some groups in the region, such as young people, the rate may reach 30 percent.)

These economic conditions are nothing new, and they are not unique to the Arab world. But they provide particularly fertile ground for extremist recruitment, and the Internet makes these young people more accessible in larger numbers than ever before. Within limits, in-person connections are far less essential given the variety of online tools available to recruiters, such as the videos described above and the online forums in which the extremist message can be discussed. Facebook, chat rooms, Twitter, and other Internet tools and venues collectively create virtual community centers that extremists can visit with near impunity.

Marc Sageman observed that rather than relying on face-to-face meetings, an

> interactive process of radicalization takes place on line, in the jihadi forums. ... Some of the participants get so worked up that they declare themselves ready to be terrorists. In a way, recruitment is self-recruitment, which is why we cannot stop it by trying to identify and arrest "recruiters." These self-recruited upstarts do not need any outsiders to try to join the terrorist social movement. Since this process takes place at home, often in the parental home, it facilitates the emergence of homegrown radicalization, worldwide.[6]

This is not to say that there is a one-step process that goes from the Web to a suicide bombing. Online material can entice and even recruit at a preliminary level, particularly in terms of finding messengers and errand-runners. This level of material, however, cannot convince and instruct; this usually requires face-to-face personal contact. For weapons use, operational tradecraft, and other sophisticated actions in which lives will be at stake, remote, impersonal training will not suffice. This is particularly true for suicide bombers. Skilled and persistent mentors are needed to instill the motivation and discipline needed before someone will sacrifice his or her life (and take other lives) in such a horrific fashion. Nevertheless, new media should be recognized as a net thrown into a sea of restless young people, some of whom will be pulled into more intensive recruitment.

The youngest audiences receive different messages. Their ranks are sown with seeds of hatred, and even if they do not truly understand what they are seeing and hearing, this "children's programming" conditions them for more explicit content as they grow older. Cartoons and animal characters are used, and weekend morning television, a favorite among children around the world, delivers poisonous doses of this "entertainment."

For those who address terrorist threats, understanding this process and appreciating its scope and effectiveness are essential if future generations are not to fall prey to the allure of terrorists' recruitment efforts.

The audience

Young people throughout the world are embracing new media. Through cell phones and computers, they gravitate to Facebook, Twitter, and even the now-old-fashioned blogs, Web sites, and e-mail that are parts of an exponentially expanding universe. As of early 2010, Facebook claimed 350 million active users.[7] They also watch satellite television channels that reflect local and regional political leanings.

The pace of localized technological growth determines how many young people in a given part of the world may enter these virtual venues; a teenager in Hong Kong is far more likely to do so than her or his counterpart in Tangier. But digital divides are narrowing, and the connections fostered by new media are becoming a more balanced global phenomenon.

By some estimates, 60 percent of Arab Muslims are under age 30,[8] which means the popularity of new media is certain to accelerate as access to it widens. The mobile phone is fast becoming ubiquitous, particularly among the young and particularly in developing countries, providing relatively inexpensive connectivity at numerous levels ranging from basic telephone conversations to Internet access. The socialization of young people around the world is changing because of this. The mobilizing power of new, social media could be seen in the post-election turmoil in Iran in 2009, and examples from China to Colombia to the U.S.A. illustrate the political ramifications of this kind of technological change. "Networking" in its many incarnations is growing with great speed and great diversity in its users and uses. Much of this is constructive, or at least harmless. But the breadth and speed of network connectivity can lend themselves to other purposes, such as extremist proselytizing and organizing with unprecedented reach and security. This is an important factor to be considered when contemplating the future of terrorism.

Much of this evolution in the technology and role of mass communication has roots in the birth of Al Jazeera in 1996, which marked the beginning of the current surge of interest in opening up the Arab public sphere. Building on the tradition established by Al Jazeera's talk shows, diverse and easily accessible media platforms have encouraged social discourse that has delved into topics that were long relegated to private conversation. Everything from government corruption to sexual mores to religious doctrine is discussed fervently and widely, and as each new technological advance offers new forums, the discussions broaden and intensify.

Social networking Web sites designed for Muslim users appeal to the desire for a community that has a religious base but not necessarily a distinct political grounding. For those who visit these sites, which are in the religious mainstream rather than extremist, communicating with one another has the highest priority. Among the sites that fit this description is mecca.com, which features this mission statement:

> Mecca.com offers a point of solidarity for online Muslims worldwide. Our goal is to promote and reinforce an inspiring, positive image of the strong values that Muslims bring to their respective communities everywhere. At mecca.com, we help Muslims everywhere come closer to achieving their own personal dreams—whatever they may be. Together, anything is possible.[9]

Another site, this one entirely student-run, is MideastYouth.com, which defines its purpose this way:

> One thing we in the Middle East know is that liberty does not come at the barrel of a gun. It does not just happen when tyrants are deposed or systems overturned. Liberty depends on the support of a network of institutions, many of which we do not have. At MideastYouth.com, we target one aspect necessary to the development of liberty and that aspect is free speech. At MideastYouth.com, free speech is more than an idea, it is a practice. We use the internet platform to practice communicating our own stories to each other while listening to those of others. As simple as it may seem to a Westerner, the very creation of MideastYouth.com, its power and influence, its underlying principles, and its hardheaded determination are radical in and of themselves. MideastYouth.com has undertaken unprecedented initiatives, including fighting for the rights of religious minorities, highlighting the plight of the region's

migrant workers, and promoting independent, grassroots journalism in Afghanistan.

The site also notes that its contributors include

> Palestinian Christians, Arab Jews, Iranian atheists, Israeli soldiers, Sudanese poets, Pakistani activists, Kurdish students, Arab Americans and many more representing different sects, social class, nationalities or religions. We strive to prove that despite all these differences we find ways to tolerate, support, and work with each other.[10]

This site's statement of purpose provides a useful reminder for those in democratic nations that in much of the world free speech is, in itself, still a goal rather than a reality.

On mainstream sites such as these, any references to terrorist organizations are usually critical. Bruce Etling, of Harvard University's Berkman Center for Internet and Society, noted that terrorist groups do not try to use these venues because they cannot maintain a static online presence for fear of detection, and sites such as mecca.com, MideastYouth.com, and Facebook police their content and will purge extremist material.[11] As these more constructive sites grow in number and popularity, they might displace some of the extreme online offerings in terms of gaining visitors and expanding influence. As crowded as the virtual world is, people have only so much time to spend there, so its inhabitants must compete for audience.

Aside from their respective offerings, these sites more generally foster increased use of Internet-based media as tools of social connectivity. The intensity of their users' involvement, the durability of networks extending from these online entities, the shifts in identity fostered by this kind of virtual involvement with others ... all these and other difficult-to-determine outcomes are factors in the development of what Manuel Castells has called "the cultural communes of the information age." These communes are largely reactive, homes for responses to aspirations and threats. The Internet affords a home conducive to nurturing strategies against perceived threats such as globalization and the resultant diminution of individuality and identity.[12] The more theoretical issues concerning the Internet's effects on societal evolution are worth keeping in mind as a backdrop to politically charged matters related to social reform. The spectrum of such issues is broad and may provide pathways for extremists to influence young people's developing attitudes about the desire for change in various aspects of their lives.

The Internet can be an anti-extremist tool as well as a vehicle for extremist proselytizing and recruitment. Mainstream Internet content may serve a de facto antiterrorism function because it can offer connections to a larger world that may reduce the social isolation that makes radicalism appealing. It should be noted that many of the most popular sites, wherever they may be based, use English as their primary language, with Arabic, Farsi, and other languages as secondary (their use usually determined by whether the site's budget allows paying translators). The MideastYouth site notes that it is in English because "it is our common spoken language, allowing us to communicate despite other linguistic barriers."

Throughout much of the world, young people have an insatiable appetite for the instruments and content of new media. Most of what they are provided is relatively benign, even from the advertisers who see new media as offering so many new ways to reach these consumers. But these media also have appeal to those who have less lawful intentions, and see new media as tools to cultivate a new generation that will champion their cause.

Why it matters

Terrorist organizations have no qualms about propagandizing even the very young. Training children is also not uncommon. Using children in operations, including suicide attacks, does happen, although it is opposed even by many clerics and others who may advocate extremist viewpoints.

A quick sweep of YouTube will illustrate the pervasiveness of this abuse. Whether the recruiters are Al Qaeda, the Taliban, the Tamil Tigers of Sri Lanka, or others, abundant video evidence shows children—some looking to be no more than 12 years old—carrying real weapons just as casually as their counterparts a generation ago carried toy guns. In one YouTube video, a little girl recites a poem: "Daddy brought me a present/Machine gun and a rifle/ When I grow into a young adult/I will join the liberation army."[13] In another video, a young Palestinian boy, holding an assault rifle, calmly says, "I send this message to [Israeli Prime Minister] Sharon that my father's blood will not be gone to waste."[14]

These are not "just videos" that can be dismissed as having no effect. Child recruitment through new media and other means must be taken seriously. According to a report by elaph.com, Abd Al-Bari Al-Zamzami, a member of parliament in Morocco and head of the Morocco Islamic Law Research Council, declared that minors cannot be used for martyrdom ("free choice") or suicide (coerced) missions. Al-Zamzami said:

> Children are being forced to carry out these operations, and this is in fact murder. Their recruiters are killing them in the name of religion. … Anyone who assigns them to carry out such operations bears the responsibility for their killing. A person who pushes the children into these battles is like someone who kills his sons.

Maher al-Soussi of Gaza Islamic University supported this opinion, pointing out that the Prophet Muhammad had refused to accept 13- and 14-year-old youths into his army because of their age.[15]

Setting aside for the moment the issue of the relatively rare deployment of children (defined for our purposes as age 15 and under) as principals in terrorist operations, more attention should be paid to the widespread proselytizing of children as part of an effort not only to recruit future terrorists but also to build a base of long-term popular support for terrorist organizations' agendas.

This has been a particular concern in the United Kingdom, where a 2008 MI5 report, "Understanding Radicalization and Violent Extremism in the UK," cited the role of online communities:

> People do not generally become radicalized simply through passive browsing of extremist websites, but many such sites create opportunities for the "virtual" social interaction that drives radicalization in the virtual world. Books, DVDs, pamphlets, and music all feature in the experiences of British terrorists, but their emotional content—such as images of atrocities against Muslims—is often more important than their factual content.

The MI5 analysis was based on several hundred case studies of persons involved with terrorist activity. It concluded that radicalization is a slow process over months or years and cannot be accomplished solely through online or other depersonalized connections, but rather requires some level of personal interaction to actually pull someone into a violent extremist network.[16]

Jonathan Evans, the director general of MI5, warned in 2007 that these efforts can be geared to recruit the young. "Terrorists," he said, "are methodically and intentionally targeting young people and children in this country. They are radicalizing, indoctrinating, and grooming young vulnerable people to carry out acts of terrorism."[17]

External factors also affect recruitment. Wars conducted by the United States and its allies in Muslim countries constitute an invaluable asset for terrorist recruitment. Draconian "antiterrorism" efforts in some countries that involve large numbers of arrests and harsh treatment of those detained may create a blowback that benefits extremist groups. Such matters affect opinion within the general population but can also be incorporated in messages designed for young audiences. Defending honor, seeking revenge, protecting the homeland, upholding one's religion—these and related topics lend themselves to simple, emotional appeals that will encounter little intellectual resistance from young people. The torture of prisoners at Abu Ghraib could be used with galvanizing effect by those who cited retribution as their cause in their recruitment efforts. Mahmid Bray, executive director of the Muslim American Society Freedom Foundation, commented that "seductive videos" about such events stoke outrage and "play to what we call in the Muslim youth community 'jihad cool'—a kind of machismo, that [violent response] is the hip thing to do."[18]

In Britain, the Association of Chief Police Officers has embarked on an effort to identify "potential terrorists," asking parents, teachers, and community leaders to be alert for extreme views or other signs of possible susceptibility to appeals form extremists. The police deny that such efforts—which as of mid-2009 had identified 200 children, some as young as 13—criminalize children, saying the effort is similar to anti-drug-use programs.[19]

As with drug use by the young, embracing extremist principles is usually far from being a carefully considered choice. Hopelessness about the future, whether in one's homeland or in a diasporic community, opens the door to anger and can make a purportedly glorious early death seem appealing. A psychologist in Gaza observed: "Martyrdom has become an ambition for our children. If they had a proper education in a normal environment, they won't have looked for a value in death."[20]

Providing a more "normal environment" can be part of the recruitment effort. The Israeli government has cited the Islamic Foundation in Gaza's "Al-Aqsa Martyrs Summer Camp" and other Hamas camps where children receive uniforms, shoes, books, and attention from camp personnel. While the children are there, say the Israelis, camp staff members "instill the seeds of hate against Israel."[21] An Arab response to this, however, is that instilling principles of military discipline is valuable, particularly because Israel has its own national military service requirement.

Various NGOs, some with government assistance, recognize how children's social environment can affect their behavior in this context, and numerous efforts—particularly related to the Israeli–Palestinian conflict—have tried to extract young people from the despair-hatred-violence progression.[22] These efforts undoubtedly do some good in individual cases, but they operate on a relatively small scale and so they do not (and cannot) address the systemic processes that help sustain terrorism.

Many extremist organizations have recognized that the best way to enter the world of young people is through the Internet and other computer-related technology. Although a digital divide still exists in many parts of the world, it is narrowing rapidly. When considering the breadth of this divide, it is worth remembering that statistics showing Internet connection rates by households can be misleading, as they do not reflect the communal Internet access that so many people, particularly the young, enjoy through cyber-cafés and other semi-public points of connectivity.

One aspect of this is the use of video games for explicit propagandizing. Hezbollah's game "Special Force" encouraged its players to kill Israeli soldiers and settlers, and provided "training" that included firing at an image of Israel's then prime minister, Ariel Sharon. It reportedly sold out its original production run of 100,000 copies in 2003. A more sophisticated "Special Force 2" was introduced in 2007. In it, players copy some of the action from the 2006 Hezbollah–Israel war as they raid Israel to capture soldiers, attack tanks in southern Lebanon, and fire Katyusha rockets at Israeli towns. Hezbollah spokesman Ali Dahir said, "The Lebanese child has the right to know what happened in the south so as to imitate the jihadist action and the act of liberating the land." He added:

> This game presents the culture of the resistance to children: that occupation must be resisted and that land and the nation must be guarded. ...
> The features which are the secret of the resistance's victory in the south

have moved to this game so that the child can understand that fighting the enemy does not only require the gun. It requires readiness, supplies, armament, attentiveness, tactics.

In response, Israeli Foreign Ministry spokesman Mark Regev said, "It should come as a surprise to no one that Hezbollah teaches children that hatred and violence are positive attributes." Dahir said the Hezbollah product could be differentiated from popular but violent American games, arguing, "We are not presenting it as a game that does not contain violence, but the difference is that the child does not play with a useless game without a cause or message."[23]

Such games are countered by games with a very different message. "Peacemaker," designed by an Israeli and American team, allows the player to act as Israeli prime minister or Palestinian president, confronting scenarios such as an Israeli air strike or a Palestinian suicide bombing and deciding how to respond. The goal is to bring peace to region, while running the risk of a major conflagration.[24]

The world of military gaming is not limited to the Middle East. The U.S. Army provides an online game, "America's Army," which is described on its Web site as providing players "with the most authentic military experience available, from exploring the development of soldiers in individual and collective training to their deployment in simulated missions."[25]

Extremist groups use all forms of media—everything from print to ringtones to Twitter and beyond. In considering the efforts of such groups, it is important to remember that they are not ragtag collections of lunatics who are overmatched by superstates' technology and doomed to fail. Many are sophisticated, ingenious strategists who understand the psychology and aesthetics of persuasion and are undaunted by the prospect of confronting the United States or other major powers. There may seem to be nothing subtle about a car bomb exploding, but the same people who wreak such havoc may also be capable of taking different routes to their goals, pulling a surprisingly diverse array of people along with them. The nuanced tactics of cultivating the young illustrate that terrorist organizations can operate on many levels.

Themes and examples

Many extremist Web sites and other online forums are designed for the already converted, and so are oriented toward cheerleading rather than persuasion. When the target audience is young people, however, a different approach is featured. To reach teenagers, an online rap video might be employed. One of the popular songs is "Dirty Kuffars" ("Dirty Unbelievers"), which first aired in 2004 and was sung by the British Sheikh Terra and the Soul Salah Crew. It was produced with enough skill to hold the attention of viewers of YouTube and other online venues who have become accustomed to MTV-quality video. Strutting mujahideen, an exploding (presumably American) truck, and lots of gun-waving, all to a driving rap beat. A sample of the lyrics: "Peace to Hamas and the Hezbollah/OBL pulled me like a shiny star/Like the way we destroyed them two towers ha-ha/The minister Tony Blair, there my dirty Kuffar/The one Mr. Bush, there my dirty Kuffar/Throw them on the fire."[26] Musical militarism can always find an audience.

Younger children are also considered to be worth courting. Hamas provides a prime example of how such groups are reaching children via a Web site dedicated solely to the young. *Al-Fateh Magazine* (not to be confused with "Fatah," the Palestinian political party) is Hamas's attempt to connect elementary-school-age children to their movement by using modern technology. Their slogan "The magazine of boys and girls, the magazine of the builders of the future," underscores the recognition by Hamas that the party must pay attention to its next-generation constituency.

The site, which is available only in Arabic, provides plenty of information for children to become familiar with the Palestinian cause. While not exactly Facebook, the "Friends of Al-Fateh" button encourages the site's young users to share their pictures, to which will usually be added their name, country of origin, and a brief message. In mid-2009, the site featured 35 pictures of children ranging in age from a few months to approximately 10 years. The magazine has been issued twice a month in London and its archives indicate that it was launched in 2003 and has published 153 issues since. Users are given the opportunity to contribute material by contacting a gmail e-mail account. The magazine features user-generated content such as children's drawings. Throughout the whole Web site, all the comments submitted by the users are positive, commending the magazine.

The site includes information about the Palestinian cause, poems about Palestine, and information about historical sites in the country. Even though it is a children's site, there are political cartoons related to events and life in the region. The site also features "martyrs," including their pictures, brief biographies, and information about the operations in which they died.

Religious stories are accompanied by cartoon drawings, and some religious stories discuss the role of women. "My Dear Girl of the Future" is a section dedicated to young female readers. This section emphasizes what it means to be a devout Muslim girl and includes a recipe. In this instance, two drawings of girls show a veiled girl and one without a veil, perhaps offering an implicit invitation to those with varied religious standards. On at least one occasion (this one in 2004), the site has featured a photo of the head of a female suicide bomber who was decapitated in her attack and praise for her as a "martyr" who had reached paradise.[27]

Al-Fateh's "Children's Links" has featured only one link, to the Hamas-affiliated Sana TV channel's site. As with other sections of the Web site, users were encouraged to contribute material by suggesting additional relevant links.

This is not a particularly graphic or otherwise unusual site of this genre, and as such it underscores the insidiousness of this method of outreach. To the normal fare of children's content is added the heroic depiction of "martyrdom." A game, a childish drawing, and a decapitated woman, all neatly woven together. For the child who visits the site even just occasionally, this becomes normalcy, particularly when it is not offset by parental guidance and when it is reinforced by the harsh realities of conflict and political anger that pervade other aspects of daily life. On a Syrian children's television program in 2006, the war between Hezbollah and Israel was a subject on several episodes because, said the show's host, the children on the program had themselves insisted that it be discussed.

Different children will react differently to such material. Some will not take it too seriously and will outgrow the ideas planted by hate-filled messages just as they outgrow their affinity for the more normal benign cartoons of childhood. But for some, these messages will take root, leaving the children susceptible, as they grow older, to related propaganda that steadily increases in its directness and vitriolic content. In judging the likely effect of such content, the presence or absence of counter-messages from family members, clerics, and others will also be significant. Sometimes, however, there is no such pushback; rather there may be support that reinforces this programming.

One example of aggressive programming is a children's show on Al Aqsa Television (Hamas-affiliated) that features characters in animal costumes. "Uncle Hazim," portrayed by host Hazim Sharawi, introduces his young viewers to characters in animal suits, but even though parts of the show have the look of a typical children's program, much of its content is decidedly political. This is Hamas, after all, and so, Uncle Hazim said, "I will show them our rights through history: 'This is Nablus, this is Gaza, this is Al Aqsa mosque, which is with the Israelis and should be in our hands.'" Although Sharawi had promised to avoid graphic scenes of violence, he said he intended to teach children about the disputed status of Jerusalem, the demands of Palestinians to be allowed to return to land taken by Israel in 1948, and other such issues. He said, "I cannot turn the children's lives into a beautiful garden while outside it's the contrary."[28]

Among the characters on the children's show *Pioneers of Tomorrow* was Farfour, who resembled Mickey Mouse. During one program he told children about "placing the cornerstone for the ruling of the world by an Islamic leadership." In 2007, the Farfour character achieved "martyrdom" at the hands of an Israeli soldier and was replaced on the show by Nahoul the Bee, who said to the child host of the program that he wanted "to continue in the path of Farfour" and to "take revenge upon the enemies of Allah." During an episode of the show later in 2007, Nahoul told the audience: "We must arise in order to take revenge upon the criminal Jews, the occupying Zionists. We must liberate Al Aqsa."[29] This is the often overlooked side of expanded television offerings—programming that was not previously available is now feeding an impressionable audience of children political material disguised as entertainment, with martyrs depicted as heroes. Such niche programming is there for those who want to access it.

After two of the principal characters—the mouse and the bee—died, according to the program's story line, at the hands of the Israelis, the next lead character was a rabbit. In February 2009, just after the Israeli attacks in Gaza, the rabbit, Assud, was shown in a hospital bed, a victim of an Israeli attack on the TV station, talking to the show's host, Saraa:

> "The Zionist enemy is treacherous, and it kills everything, but I never thought it would kill the children of Palestine, and that it would bomb the Al-Aqsa TV station.
>
> "Saraa, my will is that you tell our beloved children never to forget Jerusalem, Saraa. You must pass this legacy on to our beloved children. They must never forget Jerusalem, Al-Aqsa, the prisoners, or the refugees.
>
> "Remind them, Saraa, that we have a land to which we must return, by means of the steadfastness of the resistance and the *mujahideen*, by means of the steadfastness of knowledge and the fear of God. Tell them that Assud died as a hero, as a martyr. Tell them that Assud died a martyr's death, Saraa."
>
> [...]
>
> "We should teach our children that we have a land to which we must return: Jaffa, Acre, Haifa, and Tel Aviv. We will return to all these cities, Allah willing."
>
> (Assud dies.)
>
> Saraa: "Assud ... Assud ... No, Assud ... Don't die, Assud ... Victory is near ... Oh Palestine, we will liberate your soil, Allah willing. We will liberate it from the filth of the Zionists. We will purify it with the soldiers of the Pioneers of Tomorrow."[30]

Within a few weeks, the Al Aqsa program had a new lead character, a bear named Nassur, who wanted to avenge his fallen predecessors. He told Saraa: "I will be a Jihad fighter and I will carry a rifle ... I declare war on the criminal Zionists."[31] Al Aqsa has also shown animated features that focus on topics such as the "heroic martyrdom" of children and the premise that "we must sacrifice everything that is dear to us until we regain our country."[32]

Perhaps in the fraught atmosphere of Palestine such pronouncements are so common that they become mere background noise. There is no evidence of a direct connection between viewing such programs and participating in terrorist activities. But the overt manipulation of children's emotions by "killing" friendly characters and then endorsing carrying a rifle to be used for revenge against "the criminal Zionists" cannot be dismissed as just rhetoric. It becomes part of the mosaic of anger that Hamas and others carefully maintain as part of their political agenda.

These groups can also draw sustenance from news coverage. When the Second Intifada began in 2000, Palestinian media urged their viewers and listeners to join the battle. Nabil Shaath, who served as minister of information in Yasser Arafat's government, said, "During the Intifada, television and radio became a tool for generating resistance and generating steadfastness facing very difficult times." The Palestinian Broadcasting Corporation (PBC) dropped its regular programming and broadcast minute-by-minute coverage of the fighting. When images were broadcast of 12-year-old Mohammed el-Dura dying in his father's arms after being caught in the gunfire of a street battle, Palestinian television carried messages to young people telling them to "Drop your toys and pick up rocks." In one such spot, an actor playing the slain boy in "child heaven" said to young viewers, "I wave to you not to say goodbye but to say, 'Follow me.'" Not until mid-2004 did the Palestinian media begin to return to non-conflict-related programs.[33]

Having won the 2006 Palestinian elections, Hamas can claim political legitimacy, but it nevertheless perpetuates a struggle that will never reach peaceful resolution if generation after generation is brought up to believe that their future will be shaped by weapons and vengeance. Realists might argue that this is the true situation and Palestinians might as well learn about it at an early age. As is the case with much extremist and terrorist media content, nihilism is common and damaging. The counterargument is that children should be taught constructive, nonviolent ways to redress grievances. Debate about this is just as intense when it comes to the education of children as it is when considering what political path adults should follow.

The content provided by "Uncle Hazim" is not unique to Al Aqsa Television or Palestine. Egypt's Al-Rahma Television features young children on its programs delivering messages such as this: "Oh Allah, completely destroy and shatter the Jews. Oh Allah, torment them with a disease that has no cure or remedy. Send a thunderbolt down upon them from Heaven. Oh Allah, torment them with every kind of torment." The boy was praised by the program host: "Well done. Well done. I let him end the program on purpose. Of course, he memorized this, and the understanding will come, Allah willing. But this is one stage in becoming a future preacher."[34]

Awladnaa.net, a children's site linked to the principal Web site of Egypt's Muslim Brotherhood, has included the following items:[35]

- U.S. president George W. Bush "has declared a Crusade against the Muslim world, and our role is to prepare ourselves for jihad against the enemies of Allah."
- "Did you know that the Jews murdered 25 of the prophets of Allah, and that their black history is full of crimes of murder and corruption?"
- "Did you know that the Jews who occupy our land and our holy places in beloved Palestine are planning to occupy the rest of the Muslim countries and to establish a Greater Israel, from the Euphrates to the Nile, and they are interested in excavating the tomb of our beloved Prophet?"
- A section on the site is headlined, "Murdering Children—Part of the Jewish Religion."

Yet another example: An Iranian animated children's film that aired on IRIB 3 television in 2005 shows ruthless Israeli soldiers murdering civilians, including the parents of Abd al-Rahman, a young boy who in his grief turns to people who promise, "At all costs, we must prevent the barbaric Zionist murdering of our people." As the story concludes, Abd al-Rahman ties a string of grenades around his waist, pulls the pins, and leaps into the midst of an Israeli military convoy, blowing up his enemies and himself.[36]

Such content occasionally receives attention from the news media and organizations that monitor extremist groups. There is no evidence that this proselytizing represents substantial sentiment or that it has measurable effect. Of course, even just a handful of successes by extremist clerics and others could help produce a small but lethal cadre of terrorists. Although it receives less notice, some pushback occurs. A columnist in the Saudi newspaper *Al-Riyadh* wrote in early 2009:

> If we want to protect our young children from one day becoming fanatics or terrorists, we need to provide them with a completely new culture that is radically different than the religious, intellectual, and social culture that has dominated us for many decades, and still does. Instead of teaching your children hostility, or letting someone else teach them hostility, towards those of other religions, teach [them] religious tolerance, which will [ensure that while] they differ from others in religion, they will share with them their common humanity.[37]

Moderate voices such as this are not isolated and presumably are being heard in individual households and neighborhoods, supported by the many clerics and others who oppose violence. They may not often reach the larger world, while those on the other end of the spectrum may find their exhortations magnified and transmitted by third parties. This is an example of the difficulty of measuring the "terrorist threat." It would be dangerous to dismiss the power of hate speech and the subtle (and not-so-subtle) efforts to enlist the young into the ranks of those whose actions are shaped by hatred. But taking a holistic view may provide the balance that is essential to accuracy.

5 Women and terrorism

Women and politics

In most patriarchal societies, which represent the majority of the 192 member states of the United Nations, women have historically played a minor role in politics as compared to their male counterparts. Where women do play a role in politics, it is usually a subordinate role to male leaders. The media have arguably reinforced beliefs and stereotypes in masculine cultures about the role women ought to play in society. This includes but is not limited to the roles actresses play in movies and the way women are portrayed in advertising. Few exceptions to this exist in politics. Today, less than 10 percent of the 192 countries have a female president or prime minister. Bangladesh, with a Muslim population of over 80 percent, is one country with a female prime minister, Sheikh Hasina Wajed.

During the 2008 presidential election campaign in the United States, a country that is classified by cultural scholars as masculine, both the liberal and conservative media were criticized for unfair treatment of presidential candidate Hillary Clinton and vice-presidential candidate Sarah Palin. Gender bias still exists even in the most developed countries.

As in traditional nation-state politics, women have historically played a minor role in terrorism. Women joining resistance movements is a process in the making, not an overnight change. Their involvement in direct terrorist attacks has been limited although not absent. (As is noted below, this varies depending on the part of the world being analyzed.) In terrorism, women have traditionally played a more nurturing role, offering moral support to sons and husbands who join the movement. In Palestine, only after the first female martyr, or shahida, committed a suicide attack in 2002 and the "Palestinian street" made a heroine out of her, did Fatah's Al-Aqsa Martyrs Brigade claim responsibility for the attack. And this is how change, slowly but surely, creeps into historically masculine societies by accepting and welcoming nontraditional roles for women.[1]

Numerous efforts to identify a global profile of a terrorist have not been successful. Researchers usually zoom into a specific region or country, and based on published information about terrorist attacks in the area, attempt to find shared characteristics among those who committed the acts, be it age, gender, education, or income. Previous literature that links lack of education with terrorism has been challenged by studies of recent terrorists who come from more affluent backgrounds. So if it is nearly impossible to come up with a profile for the average terrorist, how is it possible to do the same for the average female terrorist when women's heavy involvement is a relatively new phenomenon?

Female attackers have ranged in age between late teens to late fifties and have come from both educated and uneducated backgrounds. According to Robert Pape, who did one of the most comprehensive studies in the field, compiling data on all suicide attacks in the world between 1980 and 2003, 15 percent of those whose gender was identified were female. Females represented 5 percent of Palestinian attacks, 16 percent of Lebanon's Hezbollah attacks, 20 percent of attacks carried out by Tamil Tigers, 60 percent of Chechen attacks, and 71 percent of attacks by the Kurdistan Workers' Party (PKK).[2] There is no general profile of what constitutes a female suicide bomber; however, recent studies looking at synthesizing a profile do bring up the notion of these women being in some way outcasts in their own societies. Such is the case of Hanadi Jaradat, a Palestinian lawyer who committed a suicide attack, who some argue by becoming a lawyer had overachieved in her own society. In an attempt to understand the reasoning and rationale behind the actions of these women, most in the West who are unfamiliar with the daily ordeals of the conflict in the Middle East dehumanize them, separating them from the remainder of the human race by assuming they are evil and mentally unstable. The truth is, however, these women are products of their society and all of its socio-political and economic influences. They have emerged from a very harsh environment that they were born into and eventually die in.[3]

Women on the battlefield

In Palestine during the First Intifada, women took the first steps to becoming involved in the resistance movements. While this was welcomed by those who consider themselves more progressive and interpreted it as a sign of women gaining more rights and freedoms during the Women's Liberation Movement, the fundamentalists challenged this premise and argued that women's involvement should be limited to household chores and supporting male resistance fighters. Either way, women challenged the status quo. Liberation was a movement in the making and women joining the resistance, be it protesting on the streets or doing the heavy lifting, was a manifestation of this change.

Reports over the past five years indicate that women are increasingly being recruited or are volunteering to join insurgency movements. This trend of women joining forces with their male counterparts is by no means a phenomenon of the twenty-first century. The traditional role played by women in insurgencies has been generally confined to providing moral support and attending to the wounded. This role is being challenged, and it can be attributed to two reasons.

First, women globally are gaining more "rights" and pushing the boundaries that dictate what society expects of them. The traditional daughter/wife/mother roles have been expanding since the beginning of the twentieth century when women were encouraged to join the workforce as their husbands and sons joined the army and navy, and eventually were encouraged to join the army/navy itself although in separate women's corps. In the twenty-first century, women are being more fully integrated into the armed forces of numerous nations, including being allowed to serve in combat.

We are seeing the same thing happening with insurgency groups. This is a natural progression of events and should not come as a complete surprise. Women who have historically supported insurgency groups by doing the behind-the-scenes work are now on the front lines of the movement. While not an everyday occurrence, female bombers in Iraq are not uncommon. Thanks to their abayas (the long and loose black dress), it is easier for them to hide explosives than it is for men. Since it is not culturally acceptable for male security guards to touch females, women often pass by unchecked. That was the case in June 2008 when a young Iraqi woman detonated a bomb near a crowd of football fans celebrating the victory of Iraq over China, just after she had been questioned by suspicious police officers.[4] In a report by the Islamic Army in Iraq, the organization condemned the Iraqi government's alleged practice of imprisoning female family members to entice the male member to surrender to the police. The report goes further to explain that such actions contradict the Arab and Muslim cultural standard that does not allow any interaction with a woman without the presence of a male relative.[5]

To address the growing problem of women participating in the insurgency in Iraq, the U.S. military has recruited and trained women police officers, but attacks by women bombers clearly undermine the security efforts in the country, and as of early 2010 they are increasing. At the height of the attacks against the U.S. and the Allied Forces in Iraq, three suicide attempts a month by female bombers were not uncommon.

In 2009 women police from the Nablus Province Police Department joined their male partners in patrolling the streets of Nablus in the West Bank. Pictures of the veiled officers wearing bright yellow reflective vests surfaced in Arab newspapers as well as on extremists' online forums.[6] The move, which was seen as a sign of progress and a victory for the women's rights movement by some, was ridiculed by others who felt this violated cultural and religious norms. In the Saraya Al-Quds forum, when the pictures of these women surfaced, forum members mocked the decision of the women to join the police academy and questioned their ability to maintain order.[7]

Second, women today, more so than at any other time in human history, have more opportunities to express their point of view, thanks to the Internet. In some insurgency online forums where ideas float rather freely (as dictated by the forum's administrator), women are sharing their perspective on the movement as they learn about the movement. The Internet, of course, does not change the miserable reality that is experienced by marginalized populations all over the world, especially women; it only changes how they talk about this reality. With few real prospects to improve their lives, women who already have leanings toward violent movements are more likely to be radicalized.

In late 2008 and early 2009, news stories surfaced in different media outlets, Arab and Israeli, about Saraya Al-Quds, a Palestinian militant group, establishing a women's military unit. *Al-Masri Al-Yawm*, an Egyptian newspaper, painted a grim picture of what was happening in Gaza. A female Palestinian photographer, Iman Mohammad, was able to document these women's participation in the insurgency group. According to the interview she conducted with two of the women, Um Mohammad and her daughter-in-law, Islamic jihad was not the only motive that prompts women to join the movement. After the recent conflict in Gaza between Israelis and Palestinians in December 2008 and January 2009, which lasted three weeks and resulted in the deaths of 13 Israelis and over 1,300 Palestinians, a number of resistance groups decided to train women within the context of their families to prepare families for future attacks by Israel. "Men are training their mothers, their wives, and their daughters," the women said, "We will sacrifice our blood, our souls, and our sons for the sake of Palestine, we will make a difference in our own way." While the women said they could not imagine Muslim women launching missiles on the front lines, they see training, which includes learning how to prepare bombs and carry weapons, as their way of contributing to the movement's efforts. Um Mohammad's son, who was responsible for their training, agrees. As summarized by Iman, he said: "Women combatants are a new phenomenon in the Gaza Strip [and the training] is still surrounded by secrecy for security reasons. But it is important that the world knows that women and children are also working for the cause." The message they are sending is clear: for as long as marginalized groups such as the Palestinians remain under occupation, resistance groups will continue to expand their movement, relying on non-traditional resources such as women and children, to fight for their cause and against perceived injustices.[8]

According to video footage aired by InfoLive TV, the young women, most of whom are married with children, train using all types of military equipment, including homemade suicide belts that they assemble. One young insurgent describing how the belt works added in an interview: "If, on my wedding day, the Israelis come, in my white wedding dress I will go. There will be no barrier ... there will be no barrier between me and jihad."[9] InfoLive TV is an Israeli online video operation that claims to be independent and objective, and was launched in 2007. The station was originally financed by pro-Israel European investors and covers Israeli/Palestinian affairs. In this media war of courting international public opinion, InfoLive aims at sharing the Israeli side of the story.[10]

In Tel-Aviv in September 2009, an exhibition including seven pictures of female Palestinian suicide bombers superimposed on an image of the Virgin

Mary holding Jesus was meant to raise questions about the status of these women. On the one hand they are compared to the Virgin Mary, a symbol of love and devotion, holding a baby that is supposed to be kept safe; on the other hand they are contrasted with the reality they live, which includes rage and violence. The pictures, which were the work of two Israeli artists, raised some anger in the community, especially from the Israeli victims of the attacks.[11]

Women joining insurgent movements could indicate a number of things. It could signify that insurgent groups are growing desperate for more volunteers and are now reaching out for women whose role has traditionally been confined to moral support. Some reports argue that Al Qaeda's unproductive old methods are now being replaced with new ones: recruiting children, widows, and unmarried and uneducated women. Seeing women fighting on the battlefield could also motivate or shame men into joining the movement. Another theory points to the desperate circumstances of females in occupied nations who feel the moral/religious responsibility to fight side-by-side with their male counterparts or are even motivated by revenge for a family member who was killed by the occupying forces.[12] This is not far-fetched; the number of women committing suicide, including self-immolations, after the launch of the Iraq war has increased. Whether they are recruited or they volunteer, the number of women carrying out attacks on behalf of Iraqi insurgent groups has grown since the start of the war in March 2003. According to Associated Press statistics, female bombers in Iraq have been responsible for 2 percent of the attacks and 5 percent of the deaths since May 2005. The situation in Palestine is not that different. Women have also been suicide attackers, some as young as 15.[13]

For the most part, women suicide bombers, like their male counterparts, become heroines. Their sacrifice is admired, their pictures distributed in person and online, and their stories told and retold as they become part of the resistance movements' documented history. The stories, as they are told, are not always consistent, except for the part where the martyr dies. Wafa Idris, the Palestinian suicide bomber who detonated a bomb in early 2002, killing herself and an elderly Israeli, was 27 years old by some counts, and 28 by others. The number of deaths resulting from a suicide attack also varies, ranging from killing a couple of Israeli soldiers to killing and injuring dozens.

Stories about the motives behind these women committing acts of violence are also questionable. The typical story, which becomes part of a bigger female suicide bombing legend, usually includes a patriotic woman who from an early age has been desperately searching for an opportunity to participate in jihad and the resistance movement. The story would not be complete without the part where the woman leaves for work in the morning and says goodbye to her mother, who is later thrilled to find out that her daughter became a martyr. Variations of the story exist; the mother in some stories is replaced by the best friend, but all the stories stress three elements: the martyr's personal perseverance, the family's rejoicing when they learn of what happened, and the heroic nature of the woman's act. The purpose of the story is to inspire the locals to do the same, and send a message of solidarity and determination to everyone else: "Martyrdom operations, which have become part of the culture of resistance, are not limited to men only, the dream of martyrdom entices Palestinian girls as well."[14] These operations also send a message of equality between men and women, not so much in life, but in death.

The Ezzedeen Al-Qassam Brigade (Hamas) Web site dedicates a section to its martyrs, in which a small section is dedicated to female martyrs. As of late 2009, this section contained information about four female martyrs, all of whom died between 2002 and 2006. Each martyr has a picture with the veil on, two women are wearing Qassami bandanas on their foreheads and one woman is carrying a rifle. The database also lists the names of the women, the dates of their operations, and a catchy title describing their sacrifice: "She fought alongside her husband to martyrdom, so he doesn't leave her to heaven alone," "The mother of martyrs," "She sacrificed her life to save the life of her martyr son," and "The first Qassami female martyr."

The first Qassami female martyr is Reem Al-Rayashi. According to the Web site of Al-Qassam, Reem was the first martyr in the Gaza strip and seventh in Palestine.[15] A musical videoclip re-enacting her preparation for the suicide attack was created and has been posted by a number of YouTube users online. The video shows a young woman, playing the role of Reem, arranging explosives in her bedroom and being "caught" by her three-year-old daughter. The lead singer, who is a female, sings from the perspective of the little girl, asking her mother what she is hiding and why she is leaving her and her little brother behind. The five-minute clip goes on to describe the children's confusion over their mother's departure, and ends with the little daughter seeing her mother on TV and realizing what her mother has done, finally wishing that her brother and she were with their mother. This videoclip was shown during a children's TV program on Hamas' station. In an interview with Reem's children on Hamas TV, the anchor asks:

ANCHOR: Duha, do you love Mommy?
DUHA: (nods yes)
ANCHOR: So where did Mommy go?
DUHA: To paradise.
ANCHOR: What did Mommy do?
DUHA: She became a shahida [martyr].
ANCHOR: She killed Jews? Right? How many did she kill, Mohammad?
MOHAMMAD: What? (he had been distracted by something on the floor)
ANCHOR: How many Jews did Mommy kill?
MOHAMMAD: (raises his hand and shows five fingers)
ANCHOR: How many are these?
MOHAMMAD AND DUHA: Five.

Reem's farewell message is also available on YouTube, where she expresses her desire since she was an eighth grader to engage in a suicide attack. As typical of many recorded farewell messages, the future martyr is wearing army gear, holding the rifle in one hand and her farewell message in the other.[16]

The Popular Front for the Liberation of Palestine also has a database of its martyrs dating back to 1968. As of December 2009, the most recent death was in September 2009. Currently this database includes 374 martyrs, threeof whom are women and one of whom is not veiled. Interestingly, a martyr is not necessarily someone who died on the battlefield or in a suicide attack; a martyr could also be someone who died as a result of the Israeli occupation or even of natural causes.

Mothers of martyrs

Mothers of martyrs are held in high esteem in regions of conflict. Since their son/daughter gave his or her life for the "cause," they are admired and respected. People usually approach these mothers to extend congratulatory remarks, rather than condolences. These mothers go through an internal struggle while their sons and daughters are considered heroes and heroines by society. Their interpretation of religion dictates that they will have a safe passage to heaven, but the truth is they are dead and are never coming back home. A worthy cause, yet a personal loss.

The ideology of martyrdom, no doubt, makes dealing with this personal loss more bearable. Martyrdom gives death meaning. There is also a financial reward that often comes along with martyrdom. Families of martyrs are usually taken care of financially by the organization that claims responsibility for the operation or by a martyrs' foundation. A father speaking to a female journalist about his son's recent death explains: "Do not forget, my daughter, we are taken care of from all respects. The Martyrs Foundation handles all of our needs, from medicine, to education, to housing, to personal salaries; they don't make us need anything."[17]

On the other side of the issue, mothers not endorsing jihad create a further obstacle for these organizations who are trying to recruit young men, and sometimes women, to join their movement. In a 3,800-word letter to his reluctant mother, a Muslim in Turkey wrote the following about his intention to become a martyr:

> Peace and blessings be upon you, my dear mother! I have long wondered how to convey to you my thoughts and feelings, and decided to write you this letter. ...
>
> I am grateful to you my mommy, for all the difficulties that you suffered for the sake of my well-being, since that time when you bore me a long and difficult months, and ending with the fact that I became who I became—a Muslim, a Mujahid seeking forgiveness and Paradise. ...
> Mommy, I know how hard is for you to make this move and follow this path, but the reward of Allah for it is very high, and when you hear, insha Allah Ta'ala, that Allah has bestowed upon your son the Martyrdom on

the path of Allah, do not forget the verse from the Holy Quran: "Verily, we belong to Allah, and to him is our return!" ... I'm in a hurry to get to Heaven, and I hope to meet with you in paradise."[18]

Pictures of mothers celebrating their martyr children often circulate in international media and are interpreted as a sign of mothers endorsing jihad, even if it means losing a child. If society perceives even children dying for the cause as martyrs, and a mother loses her child in the conflict, then it is safe to assume that societal pressures combined with the promise of heaven will lead a mother to smile in front of the camera, knowing very well that her picture will make front-page news.

Women in the virtual field

To mark the anniversary of the seventh year of resisting the U.S. occupation in Iraq, the national leadership of the Baath Arab Socialist Party held a Woman's Movement Against the Occupation festival. The opening remarks were given by Dr. Balqees, a female doctor, and the event was covered by the TV Voice of Mesopotamia, which is associated with the Jihad on the Land of Rafedean (Mesopotamia) Brigades.[19]

The Women's Movement Against the Occupation and Domination is a member organization of the Nationalist and Islamic Front organization in Iraq. According to the organization's reports online, the purpose of the movement is to raise awareness about women's rights, but more importantly, to link women's rights to the right for Iraq as a nation to choose its political destiny: "There is no freedom of women under occupation, as there is no freedom of man under occupation, nor the advancement of the society under occupation." While the rhetoric is not heavily religious, the organization acknowledges the role of women as the creators of life, citing: "God entrusted us with the task of maintaining the human race to preserve its security and existence and its future goals in free and dignified lives."[20] This organization is an example of voices of women surfacing on the Internet. Generally most forums are dedicated to issues concerning males, including fighting the enemies and jihad. However, on some sites women have their own discussion threads.

Online discussions on terrorist sites continue to be dominated by males, although female voices are slowly but surely being heard. In this world of extremism, online celebrities take a life of their own where they are followed and respected by fellow forum users and movement supporters, such as "Irhabi 007" ("Terrorist 007"), the 22-year old Londoner whose identity was exposed after two years of hacking and propagandizing online for Al Qaeda affiliates.

One female celebrity goes by the pseudonym "Sister Harb" ("Sister War"). Sister Harb is an active moderator and user of multiple political and religious forums. According to her online profiles, she resides in Finland. Her online contributions range from discussing political issues including the Palestinian–Israeli conflict and the Iraq War to contributing to cultural forums on Finnish cuisine by sharing a Finnish apple pie recipe.[21] Sister Harb is a "super moderator" at Al-Moltaqa with over 13,000 posts since October 2006. She is a moderator at Eye on Palestine Forum with over 43,000 posts since March 2008,[22] a moderator of Islamic View, where she also got happy birthday wishes on November 16, 2009,[23] a junior member at Turn to Islam Forum with 880 posts since November 2006, and finally an active member on Mahjoob.com with over 200 posts since July 2006.[24] Often her posts link back to Al-Moltaqa, which is where she now contributes most of her posts. She is an example of a pervasive female voice online who contributes both social and political content to these public forums.

Content targeting women usually falls under the umbrella of family issues. While some of it relates to jihad, most of it covers generic content. Al-Jamaa Al-Islamiya's site has a section titled "Family Matters," which is not an unusual title. In this section, male authors, including sheikhs, write about women's issues. Typical articles discuss the role of women in the Islamic society. These articles start off by praising devout Muslim women, emphasize their role in the family as mothers, and stress the importance of focusing on the family. One article goes further to dismiss the notion of joining the workforce, which the author argues results in marital problems and children misbehaving. Other topics include the negative influence of Hollywood's movie industry in terms of its overtly sexual portrayal of women, and the significance of wearing the veil as a sign of religiousness and modesty.[25]

In an article titled "The Palestinian Women Have the Credit to Take a Nobel Prize in Resisting the Aggression," Al-Qassam describes the will and power of Palestinian women to sacrifice themselves and stand up against the occupying force that is killing their sons and children. Writing about Fatima Omar, a 57-year-old martyr, the author says:

> Fatima was not fed up with life and went to kill herself, but she went to resist the many killings of the children and women in the Palestinian land. She saw the occupation forces when they devastate homes, kill children, and demolish everything.

The message is clear; while women have not been traditionally engaged in armed combat, few women have chosen the route of suicide terrorism, and these women are being honored by their society, and commended for their sacrifice to the state of Palestine. Their contribution is viewed as a "new tactic of the resistance to the occupation forces."[26]

Today the Ansar al-Islam (Supporters of Islam) discussion board is no longer open to the public. A note on the Web site from the administrator reads "Closed forever" without providing an explanation. When the discussion board was open earlier in 2009, the Family Forum tab included sections dedicated to women's issues on makeup, fashion, and home décor, where random information was posted by subscribers to the forum, including a link to Neiman Marcus men's pyjamas.

Al-Boraq has a discussion forum titled "Muslim family matters: Discussing issues concerning women and children and the challenges facing the Muslim family." The purpose of this forum is to discuss issues of concern to Muslim families where users usually ask a question relating to behavior and whether it is acceptable for Muslims to engage in this behavior, such as watching movies where actresses act immorally or listening to non-religious music. The user poses a question such as: "What is the ruling [religious ruling] on watching sitcoms and movies?" The answer, which is usually provided by the same user, copies material on the same topic from different Islamic sites and credits the sources. In the case of watching sitcoms and movies, the ruling according to this user is Muslims should not waste their time watching movies that do not have an Islamic religious content, and should not expose themselves to corrupt acts where the movie characters develop immoral relationships. Other users reply to the thread by commending the "discussion," which is clearly one-way, and blessing the user who initiated the thread.[27] Such "discussions" are typical of these forums where a one-sided approach is used to dictate the discourse, which is heavily conservative.

Similar questions posed include the negative influence of music on the individual and the ruling that Muslims should not be listening to non-religious songs. A number of discussions revolve around sharing advice and best practices on how to deal with teenage children, best practices with children based on the experience of a father user, rules governing the mixing of sexes in the same room such as a classroom and avoiding such situations, advice to those about to get married and the importance of choosing a good Muslim partner ... etc. While all this content targets women, most of it is posted by male users who use the forum to educate young women and mothers on how to be good Muslims.

Few posts boast about women's achievements in the workforce. On Al-Moltaqa's site, one apparently Turkish user had posted an article and pictures about the first Turkish woman to design a mosque in the country, and other users bragged about the beautiful design and her inspirational work.[28]

Among the more relevant discussions are those about jihad and the role of women on the battlefield. The Army of Saad bin Abi Waqas' Web site has a female contributing author named Um Omar Al-Farooq (the mother of Omar Al-Farooq). Her article, "The Levels of Jihad in the Name of Allah" is addressed to female readers. Um Omar identifies four levels of jihad: personal jihad, the devil's jihad, the jihad of infidels and hypocrites, and the jihad of aggressors and those who perpetrate injustice. The third and fourth categories include subcategories that involve the use of violence. Terrorism is a manifestation of these subcategories described by Um Omar.[29]

Another article posted by Um Omar discusses the centrality of jihad in Islam (clearly according to an extremist interpretation of Islam). A female author is perhaps used as an authoritative figure for female audiences who may be hesitant about the role of jihad in Islam and the possibility of losing a loved one to jihad. The use of a female voice is an alternative to the male voices to which these women have been accustomed.

As is evident from the online forums, not everyone agrees on the religious legality of women joining insurgency groups or committing suicide attacks. In a thread titled "The role of the Muslim woman in jihad," the author cites the different types of jihad of which Muslim women have historically been a part. The first kind is direct jihad including fighting on the battlefield and nursing soldiers to health. The second type is indirect jihad, which includes encouraging a woman's sons to join jihad, raising her children according to the principles of Islam and teaching them to love martyrdom for God, obeying her husband and doing what is in his best interest and the best interest of their religion, promoting virtue and preventing vice, replying to those promoting women's liberation regarding their religious duties, and finally, advising other women to do the same by following her path.[30]

Some women are interested in being on the battlefield. When some of Hezbollah's women expressed their interest in fighting in the movement, the response they got was that "War is for men. As for women, their role is food preparation and meeting the needs of young people." In an interview with Hezbollah's women, however, they reassured the interviewee that "if there is a religious mandate for women to go to the battlefield, we are ready, we will all go." While Hezbollah's women are not yet fighting on the battlefield, they do help indirectly with "the transfer of weapons and information, communications, and other monitoring activities." In a 2004 conference of the group, one of the recommendations was to strengthen the political representation of women; a move, perhaps, toward equality between the two sexes.[31]

In December 2009, numerous media sites reported that Umaima, the wife of Ayman al-Zawahiri, Al Qaeda's second-in-command, issued a statement online via As Sahab for the first time addressing Muslim women. In her statement titled "To Muslim Sisters," she addressed three audiences: Muslim women in the Islamic world, Muslim women prisoners, and Muslim women worldwide. Umaima urged women to refrain from joining jihad, explaining that for women it is not easy to be going out with men without the presence of a "mohrem" (a male guardian, usually brother, father, or husband). She further clarified that jihad is a must for all Muslims, men and women, and that women need to support their religion in any way possible, including financially and morally, by leaking information to the mojahideen, and even by becoming a martyr. She also addressed the importance of adhering to the veil in spite of Western pressures for Muslim women to remove the veil. She asked that women raise their sons to be good Muslims who love jihad and urge their husbands and sons to join the movement. Furthermore she sent a message of solidarity to the Muslim women who are serving time in jails. In this unprecedented message, which was aimed at women in a number of countries including Iraq, Palestine, Afghanistan, Somalia, and Chechnya, it appears that Umaima's real goal was to reassure the world that those who are fighting for the cause are alive and well, while at the same time boosting the morale of the fighters.

This is an interesting development, since in April 2008 Ayman al-Zawahiri, her husband, posted an audio recording on extremist sites insisting that the group does not include women, whose role is confined to housewife duties. For groups like Al Qaeda who rely on holy scriptures to justify and advance their goals, the continuous reinterpretation of the Qur'an becomes especially handy in such situations. According to the *Asharq Al-Awsat* newspaper, Umaima's first husband, who was also a leader in Al Qaeda, was killed in 2002 in Afghanistan. Likewise, her current husband's wife and three children were killed in Afghanistan as a result of an American raid on the homes of the fighters.[32]

There are many who brag about women joining armed resistance movements, their achievements, their young age, and the heroic sacrifice they make for their cause. "Force of 17," a user on the "Yards of Arab Aviation" forum, posted an article titled "Palestinian Female Martyrs" in which he shared the profile of a number of female suicide bombers. Wafa' Idris from Al-Aqsa Martyrs committed a martyrdom operation in January 2002, and killed one "Zionist." In May of 2003, Hiba blew herself up in Afula and killed three Israeli soldiers in the process. At Maxim's restaurant in Haifa, Hanadi Jaradat, the lawyer, committed an attack with great ramifications in October of the same year, killing over 20 "Zionists." Such is the rhetoric on these forums. These women are perceived as heroines, the occupation legitimizes their motives, and they go down in Palestinian history books as martyrs.[33] Online, stories can be framed and reframed to reinforce this version of their story.

The Web is also a perfect place to share photos, even on social sites. The very pink Arabic site, "A Touch of Love: A Woman's Forum" is host to a number of photos of the "women of resistance in Gaza." The photos reveal women of varying ages ranging from early 20s to late 50s, carrying both rifles and rocket-propelled grenades, representing a number of organizations including Saraya Al-Quds and Al-Qassam.[34] These photos are available on a number of other forums. What often happens in these cases is that users copy and paste the information they find interesting and relevant into other discussion rooms, thus within a few hours spreading a consistent message online.

Some Web sites boast about women participating in the movement, and use operations involving women to strengthen their position against the occupiers. In a link to a Turkish news release posted on Al-Moltaqa's site, a Palestinian girl is seen to knife an Israeli officer at a checkpoint (although the stabbing is not clearly visible in the video).[35] On Al-Moltaqa's forum, this item is shared with other users to showcase what the resistance movements are doing. The story is framed in a positive light. While on the Turkish channel, the same story is newsworthy and it is covered from an objective standpoint, detailing the known facts about the incident.

While the enthusiasts for women's involvement are many, there are those who disagree openly. In a post titled "The role of women in jihad and defending the homeland," a male author challenges the notion of women joining the battlefield, arguing that by doing so, women are breaking Islamic laws governing their behavior among men. Other users who support this argument use quotes from religious figures which clarify that jihad is not meant for children or women. Others disagree, arguing that "In the present day, jihad is an individual's duty and salvation," meaning it is everyone's duty.[36]

The war of images

To the West, nothing is more shocking than seeing a picture of Reem Al-Rayashi, a twenty-something-year-old Palestinian woman, veiled, in army uniform, holding her son on one arm and a rifle on the other, all while reading her farewell message to the camera before she engages in the first Qassami suicide attack by a woman. Women like Reem play a dual role that for most of us is very hard to comprehend: the bearer of life is also the destroyer of life. Reem's story made headlines, with journalists wondering how a woman could possibly make the decision to take her own life and that of others while orphaning her two young children. Reem and Al-Qassam got exactly what they were hoping for: media attention.

These events send a series of messages to their audiences. In the case of female Palestinian suicide bombers, they are sending a message to the locals that the resistance movement has reached a new level; no one is safe and everyone needs to be trained. The male role is forced to adapt to new ideals as husbands and sons now take responsibility for training their mothers, wives, and children. For the enemy, the message is clear: the insurgency will not give up and will continue to grow and build strength as women and children join the movement. To neighboring Arab countries, the message is that of shaming: Palestinians are dying while their neighbors watch as women join insurgency groups. The shock value of the event is what creates the most buzz, especially for international audiences who cannot begin to imagine what is going through the minds of these young women and what motivates them to end their lives so tragically. In this war of media, images are everything, and the Web creates the platform where it is possible for these images to circulate instantly around the globe. The picture of women fighters is shocking, especially veiled Muslim women. Thus the organizations gain a victory, by both expanding their military base and making world news.

Indications are that increasing numbers of women are joining resistance movements: "female involvement with terrorist activity is widening ideologically, logistically, and regionally."[37]

The Islamic Army in Iraq writes: "Jihad is comprehensive worshiping," and reiterates that Jihad can be done by men and women, adults and children.[38] With such interpretations of jihad becoming more readily acceptable, a woman joining the movement is a natural and expected consequence.

6   Terrorism's online future

To understand the future of terrorism online, it is important to first identify the real reason behind young and old men and women killing themselves for the sake of a cause. While not everyone agrees, Robert Pape, who has done extensive research on this topic, puts forward a compelling argument that foreign occupation is a primary cause of suicide terrorism. It is not the only cause, nor is it a requirement for suicide attacks. However, if we look at countries generating attacks over the past 20 plus years and the number of troops stationed in these countries, a direct link can be seen. "There is no evidence there were any suicide-attack organizations lying in wait in Iraq before our [United States] invasion. What is happening is that the suicide terrorists have been produced by the invasion."[1] As a point of reference, the United States alone maintains a global military presence, in 144 countries worldwide, ranging from "one Marine in Sierra Leone to an Army Corps in Germany."[2]

In opposing foreign occupation, traditionally organizations such as Al Qaeda have been viewed as legitimate political movements, one of the few standing against Israel in Palestine and Lebanon and against the United States in Iraq and Afghanistan. Public opinion, however, is changing, and some now differentiate between Al Qaeda's agenda of reestablishing a Caliphate by waging a war against the West and its allies, and other Palestinian resistance movements which are still considered legitimate.

In Chapter 1, we discussed the profile of a terrorist. At the heart of terrorist actions is a larger political goal that the group feels can no longer be achieved without the use of violence. Injustices around the world fuel such actions. While not every marginalized country has harbored terrorists, nor has every terrorist been a member of a marginalized community, there is a strong link between the two. To address modern terrorism, stronger bridges need to be built between nations, ones that are built on mutual respect and interest.

Terrorist groups are doing their part to ensure that their message is heard. The media battle for winning the hearts of the *ummah*, to which al-Zawahiri referred in 2005,[3] extends to the Internet. Chapter 2 discussed Al Qaeda's shying away from a centralized online media operation and instead embracing a more laissez faire approach. The Internet is viewed as a perfect medium, one with a far reach that affords anonymity and where recruitment becomes self-recruitment.

One counterterrorism expert observed that without the media, Osama bin Laden would be just a grouchy old man in a cave. The Cold War lasted almost a half-century, and we believe that because of new media, the battle against terrorism will be equally prolonged. Terrorists' use of media continues to evolve and there are a growing number of examples of attempting to use interactivity features online, such as forums and chats. This updated use of the Web alters traditional organizational dynamics and could foster greater virtual cohesion within terrorist organizations.

This chapter will look at the 2009 Christmas Day attempted bombing and its connection to the Internet, research on the radicalization process, and the migration from Web 1.0 to Web 2.0 applications. It will then offer conclusions based on recent trends observed in the terrorism world.

The Christmas Day 2009 attempted bombing

As the writing of this book was drawing to a close, a 23-year-old Nigerian, the London-educated son of a former chairman of a Nigerian bank, allegedly attempted to blow up a Detroit-bound airplane on Christmas Day. Instead of pursuing his MBA in Dubai, which was the original plan he had worked out with this father, Umar Farouk Abdulmutallab moved to Yemen to study an extremist version of Islam. *Newsweek* reported that in an unexpected twist, Anwar al-Awlaki, an American-born Yemeni Muslim cleric who preaches extremism[4] and whose lectures Umar had attended, wrote in early October 2009 on his Web site: "Could Yemen be the next surprise of the season?"[5] It could indeed, and as Umar's story unfolded, it turned out that the Internet had played a role in his radicalization process. As early as 2005, messages posted by Umar on Islamic forums revealed his tendency to participate in jihad. Not only did Umar use these forums to share his aspirations, he also shared his loneliness with his fellow forum members.[6] Loneliness in his case was solved by attracting "friends" prepared to manipulate him. That is not to say that loneliness is a prerequisite for terrorism, but it is one factor in many that contributes to the radicalization process.

As it becomes clear from Umar's story, Umar did not join an Islamic extremist forum and decide to carry out a terrorist attack the next day. What happened in the case of Umar is a growing trend, one that involves an average Western-educated young male, who perhaps by virtue of traveling abroad is confronted with all kinds of questions about the status of Islam and Muslims around the world. Injustices prevail, and situations like the existence of the Guantanamo prison add insult to injury, as was evident by messages Umar posted on forums referencing the unfair treatment of Muslims in that facility. Thanks to the extremist views and lectures he was exposed to in London, these feelings of wanting to do something for this distant cause were strengthened. The online forums provided an outlet for sharing his by now extremist jihadist vision, an outlet where his thoughts were encouraged, reinforced, and intensified. University of Michigan students analyzed Umar's contributions to the online forum Gawaher.com and concluded that "'Farouk1986' entered an existing network which appeared to increase the salience of religion in his life."[7] This conclusion is consistent with the theory that the Internet did indeed play a part in reinforcing his beliefs. His feelings of loneliness and alienation were understandable; not many in London would agree with his version of reality. Deciding to move to a country like Yemen (or Egypt or Saudi Arabia, which he was contemplating) is the next natural step in this multifaceted process of radicalization: need meets opportunity.

And thus the Internet cannot be fully blamed for what happened on December 23, 2009. The Internet did, however, act as a catalyst for fostering extremist ideology and aided, along with all the other factors mentioned, in the process of radicalization where likeminded individuals find a home away from their homes. Umar's online contributions also reveal that "the network of 'Farouk1986' grows increasingly stable once established,"[8] meaning he had a consistent network of "friends."

This is the case of Umar, which seems to reflect a growing trend. In some cases, however, it is believed that the Internet has played a more significant role. Officials indicated that the 2004 Madrid bombers were inspired by an Al Qaeda related Web site which called for multiple attacks on Spain.[9] A Norwegian research center revealed a document they had found in the archives of a jihadist Web site in late 2003 alluding to an attack in Spain. Authorities were quick to link the two, which is very tempting to do, although conclusions are not definitive. If this connection is accurate, theoretically speaking, the death toll of 190 could have been avoided had intelligence agencies been monitoring extremist sites systematically and identifying potential threats. Realistically speaking, however, the situation is far more complicated. There are thousands of sites that are active and update their content on a regular basis. On these sites, hundreds of attacks are encouraged on a daily basis, making it nearly impossible for the intelligence community to swiftly move through these messages and distinguish between noise and real threats. As in the case of Madrid, it is difficult to establish a definite link between online advocacy and real life events. The Internet and these sites are growing, yet thanks to a dwindling economy, resources to monitor and combat them are limited, if not shrinking.

The radicalization process

Homegrown terrorism became a real concern in the United States, especially after Kevin Lamar James, an American prisoner, shocked authorities by founding a radical Islamist group called Jamiyyat Ul Islam Is Saheeh (JIS) from his cell in California's Folsom Prison. The purpose of the group, which in Arabic means "Assembly of Authentic Islam," was to violently fight the enemies of Islam, including the United States. In 2009, James was sentenced to 16 years in federal prison for his role in planning attacks against U.S. and Israeli targets.

In an effort to understand terrorism post-9/11, the New York Police Department (NYPD) developed a radicalization process model based on two years' worth of research which looked at homegrown terrorism in the West. This path to radicalization includes a four-step process: Pre-Radicalization, Self-Identification, Indoctrination, and Jihadization.[10]

The United States Senate Committee on Homeland Security and Governmental Affairs was simultaneously holding a series of hearings to address the threat of homegrown terrorism, the use of the Internet by extremist groups, and other serious concerns. Based on the findings of the NYPD, the Senate Committee did its own analysis on how the radicalization steps play out.

In the Pre-Radicalization and Self-Identification stages, the individual is learning more about extremist Islamist ideology and is searching the Internet for answers: "Once individuals start exploring, the terrorists' coordinated online media campaign provides ready access to the core enlistment message, which is meant to appeal to those who may be asking questions about their background or heritage." Regardless of the Web site, the message is relatively consistent and revolves around the following rationale: the United States is at war with Islam and there is a need for Muslims to use violent means to defend their religion. This rationale is almost always coupled with a theological explanation which is at best an extremist interpretation of Islam. The Committee accurately points out that on these Web sites "there is little, if any, room for debate; just the opportunity to learn more about why a call to violent action is supposedly consistent with religious principles."[11] This, in fact, is good news for counterterrorism purposes. It is this lack of genuinely open debate online that limits the potential of the Internet being an even more dangerous radicalization tool. This point will be revisited later in this chapter.

Once the individual is on board with this extremist ideology, the Web sites conveniently provide the user with numerous suggestions on how they could contribute to jihad. This is the Indoctrination step. Some sites advocate spreading the message online, which consequently results in the call for jihad being amplified. Some advocate teaching the love of jihad to their children. Others may provide information for joining the armed resistance movement. The methods may vary but the purpose is one: contribute to jihad.

If an attack is to take place during the final stage of Jihadization, the Internet is used as a communication tool for operational planning: "The Internet also plays an increasingly critical role in linking radicalized individuals with the global Islamist terrorist movement."[12]

The Internet continues to play an important role in terrorism by being used for varied purposes at the different levels of the radicalization process. The use of Web 2.0 tools, however, has not yet been fully realized by terrorist organizations.

Web 1.0 versus Web 2.0

The essence of the difference between Web 1.0 and 2.0 is interactivity. Web 1.0 is far-reaching, but is essentially one-way communication, while Web 2.0

fosters conversation and even community. The argument has been made that for as long Al Qaeda and its allies rely on Web 1.0 applications, their cause will advance only slightly, primarily by radicalizing those who have extremist tendencies to begin with. Recent trends of those organizations migrating to Web 2.0 applications have been evident on numerous sites that have adopted forums, discussion boards, chat rooms, and other advanced forms of communication. While at first look it seems that the organizations are making full use of new technologies, a closer study reveals that the hierarchical model of top-down information is still being implemented, even in Web 2.0 applications. Forums and discussion boards are being used to reinforce the system that currently exists. This system supports lecturing and discourages debate and challenges from those who question the organization's tactics.

As described in Chapter 3, most forums have explicit regulations dictating how members can act online. The list of rules includes but is not limited to:

> This forum is to build understanding and to bridge gaps; therefore, controversial issues and specifically issues related to the diffences [*sic.*] between religious sects are NOT allowed. ... Islamic practices are not to be ridiculed or derided at any time. ... Users must not post any foul language of any form (this includes abbreviations and/or asterisk). ... Any information, text, link or email address, behavior, post ... etc deemed inappropriate by the Moderators or Administrators of the forum may be edited and/or removed.

The list of regulations is long and the issues that can be discussed are limited. In some forums members are "fined" for breaking the rules and are only allowed a certain number of "fines" before their accounts are deactivated.[13]

In the few instances where the Internet is used to host a dialogue on forums, dissidents are often suppressed. A series of posts on Al-Qassam English Forum posted in 2009 provide a good example of this lack of tolerance toward debate. In response to a user inquiring about the Land of Israel and its mention in the Qur'an and why his question has not yet been answered, the administrator writes in broken English: "There was answer to your strange question but just as avoiding problems between members here I decided delete your post. If you like to know what was answer, I can send it to you via pm." The administrator goes on to explain, "Conflicts because many members don't like your habit to send here articles, video links etc. which only meaning is to show how bad religion is islam. This have been your meaning all the time. ... We are not blind here."[14] For the most part, this is as tolerant as these forums get. Often what happens is that posts deemed inappropriate are deleted all together without an explanation being offered.

Organizations use the Internet, be it Web 1.0 or 2.0, to distinguish themselves from other similar entities and showcase their rationales. In a document posted on Al-Jamaa Al-Islamiya's site, the organization criticizes tactics used by Al Qaeda while offering its own alternatives. Even though the organization does mention jihad, it encourages Muslims to seek other alternatives first, including cooperating with non-Muslims on joint causes, which is an alternative that is not offered by Al Qaeda. By doing so the Al-Jamaa Al-Islamiya appears to be more moderate than its counterparts.[15]

If the use of Web 2.0 applications were to be fully utilized by extremist groups, two things might happen. On the one hand, those who have some reservations about the organization and have in the past shied away from learning more about it will finally be able to share their concerns and get answers that may convince them to ascribe to extremist ideology. If extremists are flexible and they present themselves as such, then more are likely to join. On the other hand, if these forums are open to debate, then dissidents are also likely to surface and share their opposing opinions, challenge members of these organizations, and as a result, convert some back to moderation. Extremists know this very well, and this is why, so far, the message is quite consistent, even though their organizations may appear to be embracing democratic principles of fostering a controlled dialogue.

Facebook

It should come as no surprise that terrorist activities have spread online to reach popular social networking sites like Facebook. Why wouldn't they? The site, which is the brainchild of some Harvard friends, was as of early 2010 home to over 350 million active users with each having an average of 130 friends.[16] When Mark Zucherberg and his colleagues launched Facebook in 2004, they probably could not imagine that they will end up dealing with hate groups across the ideological spectrum lobbying for their accounts to remain active, while anti-hate groups demand their pages be removed. But such is the nature of the Internet, where what constitutes freedom of expression is constantly being tested.

The popular social networking site allows for individual members, organizations, and clubs, to set up profiles, public or private, and then expand their network by connecting with friends, members, or fans respectively. For the most part the site is used by average people to reconnect with old friends and maintain social ties with new ones. Inevitably, however, hate, extremist, and terrorist groups got the hang of it. These organizations are using sites like Facebook for two reasons: data mining and networking.

First, organizations are using the site to find data about persons and their military organizations. According to a statement issued by Israel's security agency Shin Bet in mid-2008, Israeli citizens are now being contacted via Facebook with requests to exchange confidential information for money and to join terrorist activities.[17] By late 2008, Israeli news media also reported that Hezbollah was relying on Facebook to arrange meetings with Israeli soldiers to kidnap them. Soldiers were instructed to refrain from posting specific information about their bases.[18]

Second, Facebook is being used by extremist organizations to establish their presence online and garner support for their cause as they network with friends, members, and fans. (There is always the risk, of course, that these profiles will be removed once Facebook administrators learn about the nature of the group.)

All the following Facebook material is as of early 2010. While the average user has 130 friends, Hezbollah's Nasrallah was one of the most popular online with over 100,000 Facebook friends in 2007. His page, which was infiltrated directly by the Jewish Internet Defense Force, had resurfaced in 2009 with 9,000 fans. Thanks to pro-Israeli advocates, the page was removed again, this time by Facebook staff. According to a *Jerusalem Post* report,

> There are many reasons Facebook would disable a profile or page, a company spokesperson said in an e-mail. Profiles and pages that are "fake, hateful or threatening to others, or that represent or promote recognized terrorist organizations" may be subject to removal.[19]

In early 2010, a less popular (in Facebook terms) Nasrallah still existed on Facebook on a couple of sites with fewer than 200 members on each. Yet he is now greatly outnumbered by dozens of anti-Nasrallah pages, one of which is called "I bet I can find 1,000,000 who dislike Hassan Nasrallah!" While that group has yet to find 1,000,000 supporters, they have found 1,000.

Nasrallah's Facebook account was newsworthy perhaps because of the sheer number of fans he once had online. While his original site was removed, other extremist organizations and organizations with terrorist tendencies continue to have an online presence, although a weak one in most cases.

Hamas's military wing, Brigades Izz al-Din al-Qassam, has only 19 (mostly male) fans of its Facebook page, which is not impressive for an organization of its importance. The minimal text present on their page is in French, implying it was set up by a French fan, which speaks to the true global nature, and danger, of the Internet when exploited for such purposes. Saraya Al-Quds, Palestine's Islamic Jihad's military wing, has a couple of pages on Facebook. The first is registered as an advocacy organization and uses the Arabic alphabet to spell "Kataeb wa Saraya." The organization has 97 friends and two videos posted. The first video, which was described in Chapter 5, is copied from InfoLive and documents the military training of their female branch. The second is of a young girl singing a song about Palestine. There are also dozens of pictures posted of different members of the armed resistance. As good friends are expected to do on Facebook, Al-Quds's members post supportive messages on its wall, in English, Arabic, and Indonesian, along with pictures of the organization's army taken from the Internet. The second page of Saraya Al Quds belongs to a member and unless you are a friend of that member, it has limited access. Most of the 50 friends this member has appear to be armed female mujahideen.

Wafa Idris, Al-Aqsa's first female suicide bomber (discussed in Chapter 5) also has a Facebook page with her well-circulated picture wearing a Palestinian bandana set up as a profile picture. Idris has 55 fans and no wall posts.

The minimal information available on her page does not glorify her actions; on the contrary, it questions her elevation to a heroine:

> In an editorial published on 1 February 2002 in Egypt's Al-Sha'ab newspaper, Idris was not only lauded as a heroine but her gender apparently was used as an encouragement for other women as well as somewhat of a challenge to men who may have been reluctant to participate in suicide missions.

This raises questions about the authenticity of the account and suggests that it was not launched by a fan of Idris.

In 2008, reports surfaced about a Facebook group called "'Ahlus Sunnah wal Jama'ah" distributing extremist material online, including a report titled Jihad: A Ten-Part Compilation. The group is an extension of Al-Muhajiroun, which is an Islamist extremist group that was banned earlier in the U.K. What is more troubling than their Facebook page is that British university students were fans of that page and according to a contact at Al Muhajiroun, they make up a significant portion. Widely circulated was correspondence between an activist for the group, Abu Izzadeen, who maintained his own page, and Facebook administrators where Abu Izzadeen was protesting Facebook's decision to remove his page—"reconsider your hasty and unjust decision … Inshallah [God willing] I can return to making use of your otherwise fantastic site"—going on to write after Facebook confirmed they would not reverse their decision: "You are mad. I joined this site so my supporters could add me and show their support. I am not surprised. [You take] any opportunity to stamp the ummah under your heel. This is why we rise up."[20]

And "rise up" they do. Hate, extremist, and terrorist organizations have carved a space online, and will continue using any tool present to advance their goals and spread their mission. Facebook provides free and convenient access to millions of users around the world. If Facebook were a country, it would be the third largest in the world, surpassed only by China and India. Using Facebook's power is a solid business decision for these organizations and a natural extension of their media plans.

Other technologies

In January 2010, a frustrated passenger flying from Dorchester to Ireland who was delayed by heavy snow jokingly tweeted "You've got a week and a bit to get your shit together, otherwise I'm blowing the airport sky high!!" This not-so-funny tweet was taken seriously by authorities and cost the passenger hours of investigation and his job.[21] Lesson learned about what one should not write about on Twitter (or Facebook or any other social networking site for that matter), but the real lesson here is how seriously this 140-character microblogging site was taken.

While this turned out to be a non-terrorist related case, the U.S. Army does not rule out the possibility of Twitter being used by terrorist groups. According to a report they circulated online in late 2008, the biggest advantage of using Twitter is its real-time capability. This was reflected by events in Iran following the 2009 elections there. With regular news outlets' reporting mostly unreliable at best, Twitter provided a ways for news bulletins to be flashed among Iranians. Aside from the potential use of Twitter, the report noted the enthusiasm present on extremist forum discussions about the use of mobile technologies like GPS in coordinating terrorist activities. "Intensive courses" on the use of such applications are available on those sites. Based on open source intelligence as well as real and potential scenarios, the report concluded:

> What did become clear from conducting research on this topic is that there are numerous different tactics, tools, and software services that can be used by terrorists to conduct activities that go well beyond the original intent of the mobile phone voice communications and that these burgeoning capabilities are available for OSINT [open source intelligence] exploitation. Further, there may be a possibility to profile a portion of particular cyber terrorist-like groups and their audiences based on the particular set of software and phones that the group recommends from OSINT exploitation.[22]

While researching the potential extremist threats of applications like Twitter may sound farfetched, this is truly the only way to stay one step ahead of terrorism. Relying on available information on terrorist and terrorist-supporters' Web sites is a proactive, rather than reactive, approach used by the intelligence community to counter the threat of terrorism.

Recent developments

Global polls show that fewer people are supporting organizations like Al Qaeda and continue to see terrorism as a serious threat (discussed in detail in Chapter 7). In a perhaps a desperate move in 2007, Ayman al-Zawahiri broadcast an interview in which he reached out to non-traditional audiences. Quoting Malcom X, al-Zawahiri attempted to relate to the African-American community by speaking about oppression. The reliance on audio and video tape messages continues as Al Qaeda and likeminded organizations remain at war against the West and its allies.

On January 24, 2010, Osama bin Laden allegedly issued an audio message speaking of Al Qaeda's continued war. The message started with "In the name of God, the compassionate the merciful, from Osama to Obama. ... If our messages to you could have been transmitted using words, we would not have resorted to airplanes ... " Bin Laden goes on to endorse Umar Farouq's attempted Christmas Day bombing of a Detroit-bound flight (although U.S. authorities have not established a link between the attempted bombing and Al Qaeda) which he said is consistent with 9/11's message. He further elaborated that attacks against the United States shall continue for as long as the United

States continues to support Israel and for as long as Palestinians in the Gaza Strip are suffering.[23]

The message, which was picked up by both international media and extremist forums, was interpreted in various ways. The United States viewed the message as a sign of the weakened state of the organization. President Obama reacted: "Bin Laden sending out a tape trying to take credit for a Nigerian student who engaged in a failed bombing attempt is an indication of how weakened he is, because this is not something necessarily directed by him." On extremist forums, the message was celebrated and viewed as a sign that the war against the United States was very much alive.

Forums and blogs

A pro-jihadi blog reads: "We, the bloggers of inshallahshaheed ... are a handful from amongst the Ummah of Muhammad ... that follow Allah, His Messenger, and the Salaf as-Saalih (first three generations of Islam) in 'Aqeedah, Guidance, Knowledge." Inshallahshaheed (by God's willing, a martyr) is an online blog that supports jihadi ideology with the purpose of

> reviving the love, spirit and knowledge of Jihad fe Sabeelillah [for God's sake] since it is fard 'ayn [obligatory by religion] today and our leaders, scholars, and community members neglect it for various [unacceptable] reasons. ... Naturally, it is a blog geared towards Jihad and there are not that many out there that are similar.

Actually there are. The blog is one of hundreds of blogs and forums that support jihadi ideology while trying to maintain a unique identity to attract followers: "our blog will be used as a channel against those weak and cowardly Muslims who want to apologize for what the Mujahideen are doing to the Kuffar [infidels]."[24]

The blog, which was apparently shut down on a number of occasions, was up and running in early 2010 and reads

> We are the followers of Ahl as-Sunnah wal Jama'ah (i.e. Sunni) and in this world of *unfortunate* labels, the terrorism analysts label us as the "Salafi Jihadi's" ... [Media outlets] have reported on this blog and the so-called "danger" we present on the blog even though it is only a mix of true journalism with authentic religious knowledge which we strive to obtain and impart. ... So our enemies are plenty and our supporters are plenty; and to Allah is the final return for judgment ... we have vowed to continue keeping the blog up for the sake of Allah; we ask Allah, the Most High, to help us in this endeavor.

This site was shut down because it was detected. The Society for Internet Research[25] is one of several organizations tracking pro-jihad Web sites. Once a site is identified, the Society encourages people to file a complaint with the Internet Service Provider who, based on past experience, is likely to respond favorably to requests to shut down extremist sites.[26] While this may be a good short-term solution, it is neither feasible because of the sheer number of Web sites that appear on a daily basis, nor does it address the long-term problems of online jihad.

It is no secret that many extremist forums are targeting Western audiences by using English as a primary language for their Web sites. What makes the case of Inshallahshaheed's blog interesting is that it is run from within the United States. According to the Web site and to an interview with the *New York Times*, Samir Khan, a 21-year-old North Carolina resident, is behind this media operation.[27] It is legal, and it is not the only blog of its kind. Issues discussed on the blog include recent developments relevant to the jihadi movement. Many commended bin Laden's 2010 message to the West while others proclaimed as a martyr Humam Al-Balawi, a Jordanian CIA operative who in December 2009 killed eight CIA operatives in Afghanistan in a suicide attack.

Samir Khan is not an isolated case but part of a small growing number of young people in the West who are attracted to the message of jihad. Although they may not have real ties to the original organizations, they take it upon themselves to use their online skills to spread the jihad message:

> While there is nothing to suggest that Mr. Khan is operating in concert with militant leaders, or breaking any laws, he is part of a growing constellation of apparently independent media operators who are broadcasting the message of Al Qaeda and other groups, a message that is increasingly devised, translated and aimed for a Western audience.[28]

Such forums are targeted on a regular basis by counterterrorism entities as well as hackers. In an interview with the director of Al-Qassam English Forum in late 2009 posted on its Web site, the director comments on hackers: "There are different groups, most of which are Zionist groups from all countries; they aim to silence the voice of the resistance and cover the real image of it from the whole world." When asked about whether his site is still being targeted he responded:

> Yes, of course, the most recently was few days ago when the website and the forum stopped working totally for a short period and then came back. ... There is a staff of professional engineers working around the clock to stop any hacking.

Hacking is clearly not deterring the administrators of this forum from improving its Web site and expanding its reach:

> The administration of the Information Office is doing their best to improve all parts of the media work to keep update with the technological and

media progress. The last was the new design of the English website, and we are still going on.[29]

Another real concern to these forums is the likelihood of other forums claiming their identity once they are shut down. By using a similar domain name, these fake organizations recruit the original supporters. But these supporters are warned on extremist forums under headings such as "Extremely important and serious warning to forum members. ... Since the closure of Al-Ikhlas Forum and Al-Mujahideen Network recently there were some fraudulent sites that use the same old links of the old site."[30]

Conclusions

In an unlikely move by a Taliban mullah, Muhammad Omar issued a statement in the spring of 2009 in which he banned a list of tactics that were formerly used by the Taliban, including suicide attacks that kill civilians. The *New York Times* noted:

> Now, as the Taliban deepen their presence in more of Afghanistan, they are in greater need of popular support and are recasting themselves increasingly as a local liberation movement, independent of Al Qaeda, capitalizing on the mounting frustration of Afghans with their own government and the presence of foreign troops.

But what really happened in the case of the Taliban is that they recognized that change is part of the game, and to win this war against NATO and its allies, they have to be more flexible and let go of failed tactics (and in their case beliefs). Just like a corporation revamping its image after a crisis, the Taliban is changing its tactics to win back audiences. This PR campaign relies on all forms of communication, old and new:

> American and Afghan analysts see the Taliban's effort as part of a broad initiative that employs every tool they can muster, including the Internet technology they once denounced as un-Islamic. Now they use word of mouth, messages to cellphones and Internet videos to get their message out.[31]

Being flexible is something the Taliban and other organizations have learned well.

The Internet has allowed for ideals to live past the lives of those who generated them:

> Though many of the zealots whose writings have been made available by at-Tibyan Publications [an extremist distribution network] have been killed or captured, their ideas persist, and the Internet has played a role

in keeping those ideas alive and proliferating them with increasing momentum. The organization of the Internet campaign has also helped retain message discipline outside of Al Qaeda's efforts.[32]

As these organizations become more flexible as well as desperate for supporters, they expand their reach to nontraditional audiences in their own lands as well as the West. There is evidence to indicate that terrorist Web sites are now targeting women and children. The West is targeted for both public opinion as well as potential sympathizers. The reliance on the Internet is growing, and all trends indicate that it will continue to grow, especially because hacking and shutting down Web sites is neither a serious response nor a real threat to these parties. Terrorist organizations that are devoted to their cause continue to dedicate the extra resources necessary to maintain an online presence while relying on the latest technologies, from Facebook to GPS, to further their cause.

7 Responding to terrorism

No one—in any country, big or small—has figured out how to successfully respond to terrorism. This is due in part to the elusive nature of "terrorism" as enemy. What does one attack and how does one know when victory (or defeat) happens? Those who launch a "war on terror" promptly encounter such difficulties.

Conventional military strategists might argue that if this is a war, let's kill those we need to kill and the remainder will give up; the war will be won. That has a certain appeal, and for a while it might appear to work. America's post-9/11 foray into Afghanistan took that approach, with a nice Hollywood touch added to it: CIA operatives rode on horseback with the Northern Alliance while B-52s bombed Al Qaeda and the Taliban from invisible altitudes. Stirring stuff, but successful in only a limited way. By "winning," the United States found itself with Afghanistan on its hands—a prize of dubious value—and despite killing a reasonable number of Al Qaeda (mostly in the lower ranks), the big prize, Osama bin Laden and his command structure, slipped away.

And even if bin Laden had been killed (or martyred, depending on your point of view), the victory would have been an illusion. Bin Laden is not terrorism; he is one player on a vast field and his significance has been overrated partly because governments, the news media, and the general public desperately want to fit terrorism into the template of traditional conflict in which there are good guys and bad guys, and specific results determine victory and defeat. If bin Laden is Hitler and terrorism is Nazi Germany, the war can be understood and winning it seems both feasible and probable.

But the analogy doesn't work. The bin Laden–Hitler comparison is silly on the basis of scale, among other reasons, and more importantly the concept of conquerable "enemy territory" is inapplicable to terrorism except in the most limited way: scattered headquarters and training camps that if obliterated will be reconstituted elsewhere almost immediately. Victory remains elusive.

So, what is to be done?

Military and security services

If a "war on terrorism" is underway, presumably the military should fight it. The specialty of the world's major military powers, however, is the use of massive, high tech force. If terrorists and their allies choose to stand and fight, as Al Qaeda and the Taliban briefly did in 2001, the United States or another superpower will prevail thoroughly and quickly. The 2001 conflict was an aberration; few terrorists are foolish enough to line up on a battlefield. They instead prepare for their version of conflict by organizing themselves in small cells and plotting their attacks in nondescript apartments in nondescript cities. Terrorism can thrive in such an environment and there is very little that even the mightiest military machine or the most sophisticated security organization can do about it.

The sheer number of terrorist networks defies a comprehensive response. In 2006, Eliza Manningham-Buller, head of Britain's MI5, said that about 200 networks of Muslims of South Asian descent were being monitored in the United Kingdom. Some of these groups were simply suspicious in MI5's eyes and were not engaging in terrorist activity, but Manningham-Buller said that at "the extreme end of the spectrum are resilient networks directed from Al Qaeda in Pakistan" and that through these links "Al Qaeda gives guidance and training to its largely British foot soldiers here on an extensive and growing scale."[1]

That connection to Al Qaeda in Pakistan is maintained in several ways. Direct personal contact in training camps or other instructional venues still takes place, and individuals might go back and forth between Pakistan and, in this case, Great Britain, carrying instructions. If delivering messages, as opposed to providing specialized training, is the principal purpose of the connection, e-mail or other Internet exchanges are quick and can usually be made secure. In the face of this range of methods, security agencies such as MI5 must commit large numbers of people to tasks ranging from infiltration of the networks to penetration or disruption of the online communication.

For those wanting a more overtly muscular response to terrorist plotting, there is always conventional military force. In the years since the 9/11 attacks, that approach has proved flawed. Counterterrorism expert David Kilcullen has written that in the early efforts to find bin Laden and smash Al Qaeda on the Afghanistan–Pakistan frontier, "we assumed that pervasive surveillance, high-technology weaponry, and unlimited cash could allow us to do in 2001 what no power in history had ever been able to achieve." And then, wrote Kilcullen,

> in invading Iraq we set out to remake the Middle East in our own image, remove a dictator, reform and restructure a society he had dominated for decades, transform the underlying conditions in the Islamic world, and so remove a threat (albeit a relatively remote one).

He added,

> If nothing else, our actions to date in the "War on Terrorism" have made obvious, to ourselves and to everyone else (whether they wish us well or ill) the limits of what can be achieved by military force, by American power, and by the combined efforts of the "coalition of the willing."[2]

Given these limits, the military has explored new ways to involve itself in counterterrorism and antiterrorism efforts, combining kinetic force and "smart power" tools. U.S. secretary of defense Robert Gates said in 2007 that "the Department of Defense has taken on many of these burdens that might have been assumed by civilian agencies in the past," including military personnel "building school and mentoring city councils" as part of an effort to redefine the "war on terrorism" as a global counterinsurgency campaign.[3]

It is worth noting that "counterinsurgency" has evolved to incorporate elements of "nation-building" and localized connections with communities of interest. Citing the precedent of successful counterterrorism efforts in Indonesia and elsewhere in Southeast Asia, anthropologist Scott Atran wrote, "We're winning against Al Qaeda and its kin in places where antiterrorism efforts are local and built on an understanding that the ties binding terrorist networks today are more cultural and familial than political." Understanding relationships can be more important than understanding explosives and other tools of terror. Indonesian police tracked down and killed Noordin Muhammad Top, leader of Al Qaeda in the Malaysian Archipelago, a splinter group of Jemaah Islamiya. He had been implicated in a series of devastating suicide bombings and was found because security analysts understood the connections among Afghan fighters' alumni, kinship, and marriage groups.[4]

These connections are important in understanding the dynamics and organizational framework of terrorist groups, but dismissing the role of politics would be a mistake. Political agendas remain a driving force behind the creation and sustained activity of terrorist organizations, and should be analyzed as thoroughly as nonpolitical elements are examined.

One facet of the exploratory venture set forth by Gates is a similar recognition that only so much can be accomplished through conventional military operations. The Pentagon has begun to authorize commanders "to engage foreign audiences via online interactive methods, such as texting, blogging, e-mail, and regionally focused Web sites" as a response to extremist groups' heavy use of the Internet.[5] This amounts to the Department of Defense conducting public diplomacy, a field long considered the domain of the Department of State and other civilian agencies, and which will be discussed later in this chapter.

The American military's hesitancy in defining its role is due partly to difficulties in understanding the enemy's priorities. David Kilcullen has observed that "the information side of Al Qaeda's operation is primary; the physical is merely the tool to achieve a propaganda result. ... Contrast this with our approach: we typically design physical operations first, then craft supporting information operations to explain or justify our actions. This is the reverse of Al Qaeda's approach—for all our professionalism, compared to the enemy's our public information is an afterthought."[6]

This means that military and security organizations intent on fighting terrorism must find terrain on which to do so. That battleground may be in cyberspace.

Cyberattacks and cybersecurity

On September 11, 2009, the eighth anniversary of the 9/11 attacks on the United States, an apparently coordinated attack knocked out several of the most prominent Web sites affiliated with Al Qaeda. (It was not known who launched the attack.) Two of the sites were able to regain enough presence to lash out at the "enemies of Allah" and the "worshipers of Satan" behind the attack. At around the same time, the Al Ikhlas site, a prominent terrorist forum that had been taken down a year earlier, reappeared, but the consensus on other extremist forums was that it was a phony site constructed by a Western intelligence agency. The tip-off: there were errors in some of the site's Arabic that caught commentators' attention.[7] (While grammatical errors in English versions of Arabic sites are common, errors in Arabic in the original site's content raise red flags.)

Such a flurry of activity on one day is not common, but it illustrates that, given the elusiveness of most terrorist enterprises, Web sites are high priority targets. Cyberwarfare is becoming more significant in numerous situations. During the Georgia–Russia conflict of 2008, attacks from unidentified sources shut down much of Georgia's online communication system, leaving citizens unable to access information sources about the fighting. The technology to cause such disruptions is not particularly complicated, and in one form or another "denial of service" attacks are being tested against governments and non-governmental sites on an almost daily basis.[8] In 2009, the U.S. Department of Defense created a Cyber Command to protect its computer networks and, presumably, develop offensive cyberwar capabilities. Pentagon spokesman Bryan Whitman announced that "The power to disrupt and destroy, once the sole province of nations, now also rests with small groups and individuals, from terrorist groups to organized crime to industrial spies to hacker activists to teenage hackers." The Pentagon alone runs 15,000 electronic networks and approximately 7 million computers, making it a tempting cyber-target for terrorists or for other governments.[9] In late 2009, U.S. officials admitted that militants in Iraq had been intercepting live video feeds from U.S. predator drones by using software such as SkyGrabber, which can be purchased on the Internet for as little as US$26.[10]

The American, British, and Israeli governments, among others, possess the technological wherewithal to attack terrorist Web sites at will. Governments do not do so in a comprehensive way because, presumably, counterterrorism officials would rather monitor the content of these Web sites than shut them down. The Web sites may serve as windows through which facets of terrorist organizations' structure and strategies may be observed. Analysis of this information can provide hints about operational, financial, and personnel aspects of terrorist groups that may not be available elsewhere.

Even cyberkinetic strikes against terrorist groups are more tactical than strategic. They can cause damage and perhaps disrupt operations for a while, but they are unlikely to do more than that. To truly roll back terrorism requires addressing the motivation driving terrorists. In many cases, that means religion.

Islam versus terrorism

In November 2009, *New York Times* columnist Thomas Friedman posed this question to the Muslim world:

> Whenever something like [the killings at] Fort Hood happens, you say, "This is not Islam." I believe that. But you keep telling us what Islam isn't. You need to tell us what it is and show us how positive interpretations are being promoted in your schools and mosques. If this is not Islam, then why is it that a million Muslims will pour into the streets to protest Danish cartoons of the Prophet Muhammad, but not one will take to the streets to protest Muslim suicide bombers who blow up other Muslims, real people, created in the image of God? You need to explain that to us—and to yourselves.[11]

That same question has been raised in different contexts for many years. Abdul Rahman al-Rashed, editor of *Asharq Alawsat,* a well-known Arabic-language newspaper published in London, addressed it in 2004 after Chechen terrorists seized a school in North Ossetia and more than 300 people, many of them children, died. He wrote: "It is a certain fact that not all Muslims are terrorists, but it is equally certain, and exceptionally painful, that almost all terrorists are Muslim." Referring to suicide bombings, he wrote, "What a pathetic record. What an abominable achievement. Does this tell us anything about ourselves, our societies, our culture?"[12]

Bernard Lewis's book *What Went Wrong?* blames the Islamic world's lack of constructive purpose on fundamental elements of Muslim society, such as the relegation of women to second-rate status and the intolerance of secularism. His conclusions have been fiercely debated, but his "what went wrong" question, the one asked by Friedman, and similar queries from others underscore the importance of Islam deciding in as much of a collective way as possible what it wants to do about terrorism. This also returns to the issues at the heart of Samuel Huntington's "clash" theory (discussed earlier in this book) that partly concern whether Islam wants an adversarial relationship with the rest of the world.

These matters do not pertain only to Muslims. Whenever terrorism is adopted as a tactic to achieve political ends, alternatives must be offered to wean at least some participants away from lawlessness. (This process excludes the criminally deranged thugs who gravitate to the fringes of extremist organizations. They must be neutralized in other ways.) Whether in Latin America, Southeast Asia, or elsewhere, governments and NGOs grapple with the difficulties of denying terrorists the legitimization that they may claim through religion or politics. Any solution along these lines cannot be imposed from outside; it must come from within. As Jessica Stern noted, "in the long term, the most important factor in limiting terrorism will be success at curtailing recruitment to and retention in extremist movements."[13]

Concerning the Muslim world, efforts emanating from the West or other outsiders cannot bring an end to terrorism that attaches itself to Islam. Only Muslims themselves can do that, and new media provide venues that must be included in any efforts to create an Islamic response to terrorism.

To the surprise of some, forceful words against nihilistic extremism have come from Yusuf al-Qaradawi, the cleric who is a prominent presence on Al Jazeera and IslamOnline. In a book published in 2009, *The Jurisprudence of Jihad*, Qaradawi defends the right of Muslims to resist "aggression" and "foreign occupation," but he also criticizes Al Qaeda's concept of jihad as "a mad declaration of war on the world" that seeks to "drive believers shackled toward paradise." Qaradawi suggests that the best forum for jihad today may be the "realm of ideas, media, and communication."[14]

Qaradawi's relatively moderate words came at a time when public support for bin Laden and Al Qaeda had apparently dropped in much of the Muslim world. The Pew Global Attitudes Project found in summer 2009 that since 2003 belief that bin Laden would "do the right thing in world affairs" had fallen from 56 percent to 28 percent among Muslims in Jordan and from 59 percent to 25 percent among Indonesian Muslims. During the same period, support for bin Laden fell from 72 percent to 52 percent among Palestinian Muslims, but 60 percent of Palestinians under age 30 still expressed positive views of bin Laden. Only in Nigeria did approval of bin Laden rise, from 44 percent in 2003 to 54 percent in 2009. Among Pakistani Muslims, 25 percent had a favorable view of Al Qaeda as recently as 2008 while only 9 percent held that view in 2009, presumably reflecting Pakistani anger about the violence that had hit their country. (Pakistan was the only country in the survey where opinions of Al Qaeda, not just bin Laden, were sought.) Opinions about suicide bombing varied considerably in 2009, with 87 percent in Pakistan and 74 percent in Turkey saying it is "never justified," while only 17 percent in Palestine held that opinion.[15]

Other polls that contrasted Arab and Western opinion found considerable divergence. The British Broadcasting Corporation (BBC)/GlobeScan Program on International Policy Attitudes (PIPA) in September 2008 asked respondents in 22 countries whether they had positive, negative, or mixed feelings about Al Qaeda. Fifteen of the countries had a majority with negative feelings about Al Qaeda, with the most significant majorities present in the European countries: Italy (87 percent), Germany (86 percent), and France (85 percent). While negative views of Al Qaeda are most common in nearly all of the countries surveyed, this is not the case in Egypt and Pakistan—both pivotal nations in the conflict with Al Qaeda. In both of these countries, far more people have either mixed or positive feelings toward Al Qaeda (Egypt 20 percent positive, 40 percent mixed; Pakistan 19 percent positive, 22 percent mixed) than have negative feelings (Egypt 35 percent, Pakistan 19 percent). Note that this polling was done before the most severe violence struck Pakistan.

These findings are consistent with a 2008 WorldPublicOpinion.org (WPO) poll, which asked respondents whether they had positive, negative or mixed feelings about bin Laden. A majority of Palestinian respondents (56 percent) expressed positive feelings toward Osama bin Laden, as did a significant number of Egyptians (44 percent), Jordanians (27 percent), and Pakistanis (25 percent). Of the populations polled, only in Turkey and Azerbaijan did large majorities express negative feelings toward bin Laden.[16]

Against this backdrop of shifting opinion, quiet proactive efforts have been underway—although only sporadically—to pull extremist sympathizers back into the mainstream. In Saudi Arabia, the Sakinah ("Tranquility") online campaign is run by an NGO and features Islamic scholars knowledgeable about extremist ideologies and computer technology who use religious argument to undermine religious rationales for terrorism. This project is similar to the Saudis's counseling of detainees, although the online outreach connects not with persons who have actually engaged in terrorist acts, but who sympathize with them. The conversations take place in real time or in a series of posted messages, often within a private chat room and sometimes continuing for months. After the discussion concludes, it is posted for others to read, which expands the program's reach.[17] One example of the Sakinah campaign at work is the testimony of a Saudi from the upper ranks of an Al Qaeda women's organization:

We began to fear those who spoke pleasantly and with well-based religious knowledge. We felt that people were identifying with them, and that we were beginning to lose supporters. Our commanders—whom we do not know personally but with whom we maintain contact via the Internet—wrote a warning and recruitment letter [calling on us] to intensify our efforts on the Internet. ... We began to talk with [the Al-Sakinah representatives], and it was their ideas that were of the highest priority for us. These [people] raised in me, and in many other women I know, serious doubts and questions regarding the beliefs that we held so deeply. There are many examples of this, such as the issue of *takfir* [accusing another Muslim of apostasy] against the Saudi regime, which was indisputable and which we had agreed not to discuss [with the Al-Sakinah representatives] ... After many discussions we found—or at least I found—that the religious rules that had been dictated to us [by our commanders] were mistaken, and that the Saudi regime was not infidel [at all].[18]

The Sakinah project does not connect with a large number of people, but it helps to chip away at the religious concepts that some extremists cite as justification for their actions. Regardless of its small scale, this approach has important potential. As an antiterrorism strategy, its grounding in Islam means it reaches to the heart of the self-proclaimed mandate of Al Qaeda and other Islamic extremist groups. Destroy their religion-based credibility and they will be seen more widely as mere criminals.

The Saudis are not the only ones following this plan. Egypt, Libya, and Mauritania have brought dialogue sessions to their prisons and have apparently convinced some jailed radicals to renounce violence against the state. (In Mauritania, Sheikh Muhammad Hasan Ould Dado, a leading Islamist religious authority, has been instrumental in the project.)[19] In Britain the Home Office, which is responsible for counterterrorism efforts, quietly urges moderate Islamic clerics and other Muslims to bring their voices to online discussions in which extremists proselytize and recruit.

Even with these and similar efforts underway, optimism should not be unrestrained. Terrorism will not meet its end in chat rooms. Former CIA officer Reuel Marc Gerecht has contended that even when Western political figures such as Barack Obama avoid labeling extremists in religious terms, such as "Islamic terrorists," it is important to remember that "the ideology that produced Al Qaeda isn't a rivulet in contemporary Muslim thought. It is a wide and deep river." It is important to keep in mind, Gerecht wrote, that

> theologically, Muslims are neither fragile nor frivolous. They have not become suicide bombers because non-Muslims have said something unkind; they have not refrained from becoming holy warriors because Westerners have avoided the word "Islamic" in describing Osama bin Laden and his allies. Having an American president who had a Muslim father, carries the name of the Prophet Muhammad's grandson, and wants to engage the Muslim world in a spirit of "mutual respect" isn't a "game changer." This hypothesis trivializes Islamic history and the continuing appeal of religious militancy.

Further, Gerecht argued, "To not talk about Islam when analyzing Al Qaeda is like talking about the Crusades without mentioning Christianity."[20]

If it is accepted that terrorism and Islam cannot be fully separated, Islam must be used as a pathway toward discrediting terrorist principles. Particularly in the Arab world, religion can provide a foundation for political positioning. Bernard Lewis observed that the "successes of Hamas and Hezbollah demonstrate that opposition parties can fare very well when their critiques are cast in religious, rather than political, terms."[21]

One report about the influence of religion-based messages addressed "winning the battle of ideas" and stated that the "paramount task for the global counterterrorism coalition is to emphasize that engaging in terrorism is antithetical to the shari'ah, or Islamic law," and to promote "mainstream"

Islam.[22] Support for this kind of effort has come from numerous Islamic clerics, such as the Council of Saudi Ulama, which issued a fatwa stating:

> What is happening in some countries from the shedding of innocent blood and the bombings of buildings and ships and the destruction of public and private installations is a criminal act against Islam. ... Those who carry out such acts have the deviant beliefs and misleading ideologies and are responsible for the crime. Islam and Muslims should not be held responsible for such actions.[23]

Wherever the home and whatever the philosophical substance of these antiterrorism efforts may be, it is clear that the Web is a crucial tool for disseminating the munitions of the "war of ideas." Using new communication technologies cannot be ignored in favor of relying solely on traditional intelligence and police measures. The Internet provides an effective way to convey the "soft power" messages that are integral parts of the two-track, "hard-plus-soft" approach that is increasingly recognized as essential in dealing with terrorism. An imam using his minbar to preach against terrorism in a mosque is certainly crucial as well, but the one-on-one "cyberintimacy" of personal contact that the Internet can provide (or can appear to provide) is a unique asset.

Public diplomacy and the battle of ideas

Although "terrorism" does not lend itself to neat structural diagrams, a simple overview might take the shape of a pyramid, with the hard-core leadership and operatives near the pinnacle. Those people need to be captured and brought to trial. This is a relatively small number, but the rest of the pyramid comprises a large mass of men and women of varying ages and backgrounds who range from active supporters to quiet sympathizers. Even if the entire tip of the pyramid were to be chopped off, the remainder would remain structurally strong. Working with this larger part of the pyramid should be the primary task of nonviolent antiterrorism efforts. One way to do this involves public diplomacy.

To use a short definition, "public diplomacy" involves reaching out to people rather than governments. As new media have fostered exponentially expanded information flows and pervasive interactive communication, public diplomacy's importance has increased. Superpowers do it, small states do it, NGOs do it, corporations do it, and so do quasi-states such as Al Qaeda. A striking example of Al Qaeda's public diplomacy was Aymen al-Zawahiri's online "open meeting" in 2008, during which he responded to questions selected from nearly 2,000 submitted through the Al-Ikhlas and Al-Hesbah Web sites. The responses were presented in a 103-minute audio statement, with Arabic and English transcripts, released by Al Qaeda's As Sahab media production company.

The exercise was apparently a response by the Al Qaeda leaders to their deteriorating standing within the base of the "pyramid" described above. Zawahiri ignored the most frequently asked questions, which were about the dynamics of Al Qaeda's leadership, and instead focused on political competitors, principally Hamas and the Muslim Brotherhood (although the latter was mentioned in only 1 percent of the questions).[24] Nevertheless, this outreach was notable for its creating at least the appearance of accessibility and accountability. The mystique of remoteness wears thin after a while, particularly when the competition—such as Hamas—is so much a part of public life.

The Al Qaeda leaders also may have recognized that they had fallen behind the pace of technology development. Daniel Kimmage, an analyst at Radio Free Europe/Radio Liberty wrote that originally, "the genius of Al Qaeda was to combine real-world mayhem with virtual marketing." But now, added Kimmage,

> a more interactive, empowered online community, particularly in the Arab-Islamic world, may prove to be Al Qaeda's Achilles's heel. Anonymity and accessibility, the hallmarks of Web 1.0, provided an ideal platform for Al Qaeda's radical demagoguery. Social networking, the emerging hallmark of Web 2.0, can unite a fragmented silent majority and help it find its voice in the face of thuggish opponents, whether they are repressive rulers or extremist Islamic movements.[25]

While Al Qaeda tries to adapt to the changes in the online world, counterterrorism agencies are also working to keep pace with technology. In Britain, the Research, Information, and Communication Unit (RICU), which is based in the Home Office, produced a report, "Challenging Violent Extremist Ideology through Communications," calling for a two-part strategy: "channelling [anti-Al Qaeda] messages through volunteers in Internet forums" and providing the BBC and other media organizations around the world with propaganda designed to "taint the Al Qaeda brand."[26]

The RICU report called for targeting the "Al Qaeda narrative," which it said

> combines fact, fiction, emotion, and religion and manipulates discontent about local and international issues. The narrative is simple, flexible, and infinitely accommodating. It can be adapted to suit local conditions and may have a disproportionate influence on understanding and interpretation of local or global events.

Challenging this narrative, noted the report, would reduce the ability of terrorists to exploit the social grievances of the various publics Al Qaeda and other such groups count on for support. The report said, "The objective is not to dismiss 'grievances' but undermine Al Qaeda's position as their champion and violent extremism as their solution."[27]

This British strategy reflects recognition by counterterrorism planners that new and traditional media platforms must be used in loose combination to ensure comprehensive reach of their efforts. By being assertive, it also forces the hand of Al Qaeda and other terrorist organizations that want to maintain their popular bases. Drawing the likes of Zawahiri into the (relative) open provides, at the very least, a chance for counterterrorism analysts to acquire information and insights about what the enemy is doing.

More general public diplomacy programs are needed in addition to counterterrorism efforts. The United States has been notably unsuccessful in developing a comprehensive, first-rate public diplomacy strategy suitable for the environment of Web 2.0 (and beyond). U.S. secretary of defense Robert Gates said in 2007:

> Public relations was invented in the United States, yet we are miserable at communicating to the rest of the world what we are about as a society and a culture, about freedom and democracy, about our policies and our goals. It is just plain embarrassing that al-Qaeda is better at communicating its message on the internet than America. As one foreign diplomat asked a couple of years ago, "How has one man in a cave managed to out-communicate the world's greatest communication society?" Speed, agility, and cultural relevance are not terms that come readily to mind when discussing U.S. strategic communications.[28]

Although the Obama administration promptly made high tech diplomacy more of a priority than it had been in previous years, these efforts have still suffered from bureaucratic resistance to technological change and problems of scale. This has limited the U.S. government's ability to reach numerous audiences. Creative ventures, such as providing unfiltered "C-SPAN-type" news to the Muslim world and elsewhere exist but have failed to gain traction. Instead, Cold War theories hold sway, as can be seen in the largely archaic U.S. international broadcasting strategy, and so do remarkably unsophisticated views of most online efforts. Partly because of the public's memories of terrorist attacks, the hard power approach is politically far easier to embrace than is a broader, more subtle strategy grounded in soft power.

Outside of governments, however, progress is happening. The Mideast Youth Foundation is one example and defines its work this way:

> In a region where the freedom to explore freely and formulate informed opinions are greatly constrained and dissent is neither welcomed nor tolerated, the Internet has provided youth with an avenue to break through the barriers. Through utilizing the inherent powers of the Internet, MideastYouth.com built the region's most diverse forum, where we challenge each other on a daily basis. ... Governments no longer hold a monopoly over information; together we built an independent news outlet for the people and by the people.

Among the projects with which the foundation is involved is the March 18 Movement, which commemorates the day in 2009 when Omid Reza Mir Sayafi, Iranian blogger and journalist, died in Evin Prison in Tehran. The December before his death, he was sentenced to 30 months in prison for allegedly insulting religious leaders and engaging in "propaganda" against the Islamic Republic of Iran.

> The March 18 Movement aims not only to make sure that Omid Reza is remembered, but also that other persecuted bloggers around the world do not disappear into interrogation rooms and prison cells. The March 18 Movement would like to become a voice for bloggers everywhere who are in risk of being crushed under the heavy machinery of repression.[29]

Other online voices discuss Facebook as a way to bring about digital democracy within non-democratic countries,[30] and yet others anticipate greater Internet use once URLs in the Latin alphabet are joined by those in Arabic, Chinese, and other alphabets. Facebook, Twitter, YouTube, and other online venues offer opportunities to demystify "the other," and if this can be done, some people who occupy the midsection and base of the terrorism pyramid might begin drifting away and into more constructive pursuits.

The importance of persistent efforts along these lines was underscored in November 2009 when 57 percent of voters in a Swiss referendum endorsed a ban on construction of new minarets (but not mosques themselves) anywhere in the country. About 400,000 Muslims live in Switzerland in what had been presumed to be a relatively well integrated society. The *Economist* observed that the Swiss voters supporting the minarets ban believe "that the world really does divide into Huntingtonian blocks, where one religion or another prevails, and the rest exist on sufferance."[31]

Responses to the vote were peaceful: public protests, political lobbying, and no violence. Nevertheless, the election demonstrated that religious tensions exist, even if below the surface. The Swiss vote was a sign that better connections between Muslims and non-Muslims would be useful in reducing mutual distrust, and not just in Switzerland. One of the best-known bridge-building efforts comes from some of the best-known citizens of the world, the Muppets.

Sesame Street was born in the United States during the 1960s after studies showed that early childhood education was crucial to a child's later learning. Sesame Workshop, the program's creative home, has continued to grow, and by 2010 versions of the program were seen in 130 nations, with local coproduction taking place in 30 countries. These localized versions feature characters addressing local issues. In South Africa, for example, where 11 percent of children are AIDS orphans, *Takalani Street* includes a Muppet who is an HIV-infected AIDS orphan and who demonstrates a vibrant and positive approach to dealing with HIV/AIDS issues.

One of Sesame Workshop's most ambitious ventures has been the Palestinian-produced version of *Sesame Street*, which evolved after *Sesame Stories*—

showing segments created by Palestinian, Israeli, and Jordanian production teams—ran afoul of intifada-related politics. The wholly Palestinian *Shara'a Simsim* began production in 2006, and although all the show's content must be approved by Sesame Workshop, it addresses realities of Palestinian children's lives. UNICEF found that as of June 2007 children in nearly a third of Palestinian families were experiencing anxiety, phobia, or depression, coupled in many cases with poor nutrition and poor general health. The executive director of the Palestinian program, Daoud Kuttab, observed that young Palestinian boys are particularly in need of positive messages, given the cultural pressures they face, and the program's content advisor, Dr. Cairo Arafat, said, "We want to show boys that they can enjoy life, share and participate without having to prove that they are tough and without reverting to violence." Kuttab added, "I would say 3-, 4-, 5-year olds—if we don't catch them at that early age, we do risk losing them to all kinds of propaganda, whether it's conservative, religious, or fundamentalist."[32]

Sesame Workshop is careful to avoid direct references to the politics and conflict of the region, but the show teaches lessons grounded in real events. One storyline portrayed the community working together to recover from a serious storm that had caused much destruction and loss. Although there were no military symbols to be seen, the story could easily be interpreted as representing the aftermath of the 2008–9 Israeli attacks on Gaza. (Compare this to the episode of an Al-Aqsa Television program, described in Chapter 4, in which a leading character of the show is portrayed as dying as a result of this conflict and calling for revenge against Israel.)

The example of *Shara'a Simsim* is not just a "feel-good" story. It is an example of constructive pushback against the pressures young people feel that can nudge them toward violence. Remember the cases examined in Chapter 4 about hate-filled children's programming from Hamas's Al Aqsa television and other sources. These messages cannot be allowed to stand unchallenged without increasing the risk of their viciousness taking hold in a generation that either can be the next recruiting ground for terrorists or can provide people who will work against violence.

This kind of message is also important in countries that have known recent violence that has subsided. In Northern Ireland, the increasing diversity of the population is emphasized. In Kosovo, the program appears in Albanian (*Rruga Sesam*) and Serbian (*Ulica Sezam*) and tries to make the "other" more humanized and less threatening. In addition to Albanian and Serbian children the program includes Roma, Bosnian, and Turkish youngsters. Because Albanians, who use the Latin alphabet, don't want to even see the Cyrillic letters used by Serbians, Sesame Workshop had to find a way to conduct its instruction about vocabulary in a way different from the usual *Sesame Street* method. Producers came up with a "visual dictionary" that shows children saying words without the words appearing on the screen. As they dealt with such matters, the Sesame Workshop producers kept primary focus on relieving children from the burdens of hatred that if allowed to exist without a response would increase the likelihood of another cycle of violence in Kosovo. One of the producers, Basia Nikonorow, said: "Hate is a learned trait. Children don't naturally hate someone of another ethnicity; this is taught to them or they pick it up from snippets of conversation and stereotyping."[33]

Programming such as this can serve as a model for what might be a softer companion to "antiterrorism" and classified as "terrorism prevention." Using Sesame Workshop's creations as a paradigm, similar work could be commissioned to meet particular needs in particular places. This will not be a cure-all; the child who is well-adjusted at age 5 could certainly embrace violence by age 16. But to do nothing to shape children's attitudes about cooperation and problem-solving would be to leave the door to violence open just a bit wider.

For young people and others, at no time should a vacuum be allowed to exist, because experience has shown that extremists will be quick to fill it with their messages. Further, merely reacting to extremist initiatives is insufficient; a proactive strategy that embraces innovative tactics is essential in dealing with foes whose own creativity has consistently been underestimated.

Selecting the media to use in such efforts should be determined by the audience's information consumption habits. In much of the Middle East, satellite television is the most popular medium. (Scan the urban landscape of a city such as Cairo and you'll see evidence of this in the thousands of satellite dishes.) For large parts of the world, Internet use is increasing, but still trails far behind television. Another medium, in public use for a hundred years, is still dominant in areas of the world that are less wired and less connected. Radio still holds sway in countries such as Afghanistan, and, given the realities of global terrorism, radio's importance should not be ignored.

In Afghanistan, Mullah Fazlullah, also known as "Mullah Radio," has used an FM transmitter to threaten with beheading those who do not support the Taliban.[34] This is reminiscent of Rwanda's Radio Mille Collines, which contributed to the 1994 genocide by broadcasting a stream of hate-filled messages urging Hutus to kill Tutsis. The worst thing to do in such a case is to leave such radio broadcasts unanswered. In Afghanistan, Americans have worked with Afghans to prepare their own local-oriented programming and given residents crank-powered radios so they can listen to the voices that are trying to drown out the Taliban's exhortations.

The Taliban leaders do not limit themselves to radio. Apparently with coaching by Al Qaeda's media experts, the Taliban have produced Web sites, electronic magazines, DVDs with combat scenes, and even downloadable Taliban ringtones.[35] (The Taliban ringtones are non-musical, featuring instead passages from the Qur'an.) Even as they condemn modernism on religious grounds, the Taliban recognize the military and political necessity of using the media they claim to despise. In late 2009, Al Qaeda itself began its "Al-Ansar Mobile Team," which uploads text, audio, and photographs for reception on mobile telephones.[36]

As was seen in the November 2008 terror attacks in Mumbai, perpetrators and victims alike rely on new media. The terrorists used the Internet in planning the strikes and in communicating with each other, and those caught up in the attacks used Twitter, mobile phone cameras, and other tools to report what was going on as it happened.

The examples are many. Mumbai, Bali, Madrid, London, Nairobi, New York—wherever terrorists have attacked or gained a foothold, the many facets of extremism have become inextricably linked to media technologies and networks.

Toward an end of terrorism

Thomas Friedman has suggested that at contemporary terrorism's heart is an anti-American narrative that is

> the cocktail of half-truths, propaganda, and outright lies about America that have taken hold in the Arab-Muslim world since 9/11. Propagated by jihadist Web sites, mosque preachers, Arab intellectuals, satellite news stations, and books—and tacitly endorsed by some Arab regimes—this narrative posits that America has declared war on Islam, as part of a grand "American-Crusader-Zionist conspiracy" to keep Muslims down.[37]

The results of this narrative range from the youngster in an Internet café responding to an extremist video that is based on this worldview, to a mentally unbalanced American army officer, Major Nidal Malik Hasan, who killed 13 people at Fort Hood, Texas in 2009 partly because he had heard an interpretation of the narrative from an extremist Muslim cleric.

This narrative, in one form or another, has taken hold far beyond the Islamic world, and if anti-Americanism is not a sufficient motivating force, anti-globalization can serve as a supplement or substitute. Joseph Nye has pointed out that the democratization of technology allows terrorists to do much more than sulk and plot in isolation. To counter extremists' influence, "democratic leaders must use soft or attractive power to disseminate a positive narrative about globalization and the prospects for a better future that attracts moderates and counters the poisonous jihadist narratives on the Web."[38]

Such a strategy must recognize the generational aspects of extremism, which are reflected in the use of new media. Although Osama bin Laden is the world's best-known terrorist, it was Abu Musab al-Zarqawi, almost 10 years bin Laden's junior, who most thoroughly exploited online venues. Zarqawi understood the value of maintaining a consistent media presence by systematically disseminating "news" about his activities. He may have alienated people with his infamous Berg execution video, but he established himself as America's chief nemesis within Iraq and a focus of journalistic attention. When he was killed in 2006 (at age 39), much of the Western news media treated his death as a far more significant event than it really was. He had done tremendous damage—killing many more Iraqis than Americans—and used his sophisticated appreciation of new media to leverage his position within Al Qaeda's loose-limbed international network. Although many American news organizations responded to this story with exultant headlines about Zarqawi's elimination signifying "turning the corner" in Iraq, his death in a U.S. bombing raid was merely useful, not determinative, in efforts to combat the Al Qaeda in Iraq organization.

Zarqawi was successfully targeted by a combination of intelligence work and military skill, and the American missile-carrying drones in South Asia have killed additional terrorists. But this approach will not eradicate terrorism. Every time an influential terrorist is killed, someone is certain to take his place. The ranks in the lower parts of the "pyramid" discussed earlier include many committed to the causes terrorists claim that they champion. Until extremist groups' ranks are thinned, terrorism will continue.

Debate continues about how best to reduce those ranks. A RAND Corporation study published in 2008 examined 648 terrorist groups operating between 1968 and 2006 and found that most groups ended because their members joined the political process or their numbers were substantially reduced because members were arrested or killed by local police or intelligence agencies. Military force was largely ineffective, according to the study: "It usually has the opposite effect from what is intended: it is often overused, alienates the local population by its heavy-handed nature, and provides a window of opportunity for terrorist-group recruitment."[39]

Ratcheting down counterterrorism from a military to a police/intelligence level makes sense, as does changing the rhetoric of counterterrorism. The RAND study recommended abandoning use of the phrase "war on terror" because:

> The phrase raises public expectations ... that there is a battlefield solution to the problem of terrorism. It also encourages others abroad to respond by conducting a jihad (or holy war) ... and elevates them to the status of holy warriors. Terrorists should be perceived and described as criminals, not holy warriors.[40]

If counterterrorism strategy were to shift away from a "hard power" effort toward a more political approach, the significance of media-based tactics would increase. A first task along these lines would be to make nonviolent political change seem more appealing, but that could only happen if governments alter their own institutions sufficiently to attract an expanded constituency. This is something the United States, in particular, must finally grapple with because so many of its allies have political systems that can most charitably be called "rigged." Until that situation changes, extremism, including violent acts, will seem justifiable even to many who would prefer another route toward change. When alternatives are not available, desperation can take hold.

These matters are crucial because terrorism around the world shows no signs of withering away on its own. Although spectacular attacks—such as those in the United States, Indonesia, Spain, the United Kingdom, India, and elsewhere—have apparently subsided (as of late 2009), it would be dangerously foolish to relax. Al Qaeda has shown that it is not inclined to rush its planning for major attacks. Somalia and Yemen are well on their way to becoming the next Afghanistans, with strong Al Qaeda-related activity in both countries as 2010 began.

In Somalia, the Shabab embrace many of the same repressive measures that the Taliban have employed in trying to dictate how Afghans should live their lives. The Shabab's relationship with Al Qaeda is hard to precisely determine, but they share malignant intent, at the very least. The enormous cost, in lives and money, of the war in Afghanistan could continue indefinitely, with the next battlegrounds being Somalia and Yemen, and then ... who knows where?

New media will be part of this. In December 2009, five American men were detained in Pakistan as they apparently tried to join Al Qaeda to fight against U.S. forces in Afghanistan. They had been recruited online, with initial contact coming after one of the men had repeatedly commented positively about YouTube videos showing attacks on American troops. A U.S. Department of Homeland Security official said, "Online recruiting has exponentially increased, with Facebook, YouTube, and the increasing sophistication of people online." Another apparent factor in the increase in online contacts is the success of intelligence agencies in scrutinizing activities at mosques, community centers, and other real-, as opposed to cyber-, world places where recruiting might occur.[41] Somalia's Shaba have also engaged in recruitment within the United States.[42]

As disturbing to counterterrorism officials as this story may be, the greater fear is that this recruitment will lead not to such young men going overseas to fight, but rather finding targets close to home. As was seen in the 2005 London bombings, "homegrown terrorism" is a threat that is difficult to deter, at least through conventional security methods.

Late 2009 also saw the emergence on the global stage of Anwar al-Awlaki, the American-born Yemeni sheikh who had been implicated in the shootings at Fort Hood, Texas in November of that year. After a failed attempt to firebomb a Northwest Airlines flight from Amsterdam to Detroit, it was found that the would-be bomber, a young Nigerian named Umar Farouk Abdulmutallab, had frequently visited Awlaki's Web site. As more attention focused on Awlaki, ties were also found to the men who planned to attack the U.S. Army base at Fort Dix, New Jersey in 2008 and to the Britons who carried out the 7/7 London bombings in 2005. More than 2,000 Awlaki clips could be found on YouTube, which as of the end of 2009 had been viewed about 3 million times.[43]

Journalist Abdul Rahman al-Rashed wrote that Awlaki "is the bin Laden of the Internet." Noting Awlaki's influence, Rashed argued that

"Al Qaeda" is an ideological problem rather than an organizational one. Whilst there is a lot to do on the ground in order to eradicate this malignant disease, the first priority should be to confront extremist ideology, its theorists and scholars before its students and soldiers.[44]

Awlaki became the terrorist media star of the moment, but lost in most of the news coverage of his role in terrorist enterprises was the thread of his persistent and successful use of the Internet to connect with followers and inspire them to action. Without the Internet, Awlaki would be far less of a menace.

Discouraging news about the growth of terrorist operations in Somalia, Yemen, and elsewhere continues to accumulate, but on the other hand, polling data showing the decline in popular support for violent actions, whatever their rationale, provides encouragement to those who believe that the destructive nihilism at the heart of terrorism may be receding. Perhaps the new communication technologies can help bring an end, or at least significantly reduce, the fierce threat of terrorism.

No magic formula exists to reach this result. To get underway, the best plan may be to create a comprehensive strategy that will use in a coordinated way the many component elements of new media to counter the work of terrorists. So far, extremists who embrace violence have done a better job of mastering these media, but there is no reason they should be allowed to continue to hold the upper hand.

Notes

Preface

1 Karen Armstrong, *Muhammed: A Biography of the Prophet* (San Francisco: HarperSanFrancisco, 1993), 168.
2 John Kifner, "Massacre Draws Self-Criticism in Muslim Press," *New York Times*, September 9, 2004.

1 Communicating terror

1 Steven R. Corman, Angela Trethewey, and H. L. Goodall, Jr. (eds.), *Weapons of Mass Persuasion: Strategic Communication To Combat Violent Extremism* (New York: Peter Lang, 2008), 6.
2 National Counterterrorism Center, *2008 Report on Terrorism* (April 30, 2009), http://wits.nctc.gov/ReportPDF.do?f=crt2008nctcannexfinal.pdf, 10, 12.
3 National Counterterrorism Center, *2008 Report on Terrorism*, 4.
4 U.S. Code, Section 2656f(d) (2007).
5 U.S. Department of Defense, *Department of Defense Dictionary of Military and Associated Terms*, www.dtic.mil/doctrine/jel/new_pubs_/jp1_02, accessed July 7, 2009.
6 United States Senate Committee on Homeland Security and Governmental Affairs, "Violent Islamist Extremism, the Internet, and the Homegrown Terrorist Threat," May 8, 2008, 12.
7 Karen Armstrong, *Muhammad* (San Francisco: HarperSanFrancisco, 1993), 168.
8 William McCants, "Militant Ideology Atlas," U.S. Military Academy Combating Terrorism Center, November 2006, 5.
9 Bruce Hoffman, *Inside Terrorism* (New York: Columbia University Press, 1998), 44.
10 Lawrence Wright, *The Looming Tower: Al Qaeda and the Road to 9/11* (New York: Knopf, 2006), 4.
11 Michael Walzer, *Just and Unjust Wars* (New York: Basic Books, 1977), 197.
12 Gilles Kepel, *Beyond Terror and Martyrdom* (Belknap/Harvard, 2008), 89–90.
13 Parts of the following section have appeared in different form in Philip Seib, *The Al Jazeera Effect* (Dulles, VA: Potomac Books, 2008).
14 Susan Sontag, "First Reactions," *New Yorker*, September 24, 2001, 42.
15 Bethami A. Dobkin, *Tales of Terror: Television News and the Construction of the Terrorist Threat* (Westport, CT: Praeger, 1992), 52.
16 Joseph S. Tuman, *Communicating Terror: The Rhetorical Dimensions of Terrorism* (2nd edition) (Los Angeles: Sage, 2010), 196.
17 Brigitte L. Nacos, *Mass-Mediated Terrorism* (2nd Edition) (Lanham, MD: Rowman & Littlefield, 2007), 15.

18 www.snopes.com/rumors/reuters (accessed June 28, 2009).
19 Brooke Barnett and Amy Reynolds, *Terrorism and the Press: An Uneasy Relationship* (New York: Peter Lang, 2009), 55.
20 www.guardian.co.uk/styleguide
21 Clark Hoyt, "Separating the Terror and the Terrorists," *New York Times*, December 13, 2008.
22 Michael Getler, "The Language of Terrorism," *Washington Post*, September 21, 2003.
23 Manuel Castells, *The Power of Identity* (2nd edition) (Malden, MA: Blackwell, 2004), 139.
24 Philip Seib, "The News Media and the 'Clash of Civilizations,'" *Parameters*, XXIV, no. 4 (Winter 2004–05), 71–85.
25 Patrick E. Tyler and Don Van Natta, Jr., "Militants in Europe Openly Call for Jihad and Rule of Islam," *New York Times*, April 26, 2004.
26 Bernard Lewis, "The Roots of Muslim Rage," *Atlantic Monthly*, September 1990.
27 Samuel P. Huntington, "The Clash of Civilizations?" *Foreign Affairs*, 72 (Summer 1993), 22.
28 Samuel P. Huntington, *The Clash of Civilizations and the Remaking of World Order* (New York: Simon and Schuster, 1996), 20.
29 CNN interview with Peter Arnett, March 1997, "Transcript of Osama bin Laden interview by Peter Arnett," http://news.findlaw.com/cnn/docs/binladen/binlade-nintvw-cnn.pdf; ABC interview with John Miller, May 1998, www.pbs.org/wgbh/pages/frontline/shows/binladen/who/interview.html
30 Adeed Dashwa, "Arab Nationalism and Islamism: Competitive Past, Uncertain Future," *International Studies Review*, 2 (Fall 2000), 89.
31 Ervand Abrahamian, "The U.S. Media, Samuel Huntington, and September 11," *Middle East Report*, no. 223 (Summer 2002), 62.
32 Mustafa Ceric, "Islam Against Terrorism," speech delivered to the Euro-Atlantic Partnership council, Vienna, Austria, June 14, 2002.
33 Shibley Telhami, "Manipulating Elections Is Not an Al Qaeda Goal," *Daily Star*, July 26, 2004.
34 National Commission on Terrorist Attacks, *The 9/11 Commission Report* (New York: W. W. Norton, 2004), 375.
35 Philip Seib, *The Al Jazeera Effect* (Washington, DC: Potomac, 2008), 83.
36 Jakob Skovgaard-Petersen, "The Global Mufti," in Birgit Schaebler and Leif Stenberg (eds.), *Globalization and the Muslim World* (Syracuse, NY: Syracuse University Press, 2004), 155–56.
37 Jon W. Anderson, "New Media, New Publics: Reconfiguring the Public Sphere of Islam," *Social Research*, 70, no. 3 (Fall 2003), 898.
38 Gilles Kepel, *The War for Muslim Minds* (Cambridge, MA: Harvard University Press, 2006), 19.
39 Anthony Shadid, *Legacy of the Prophet* (Boulder, CO: Westview, 2002), 68; Marc Lynch, "Al Qaeda's Media Strategies," *The National Interest*, 2006.
40 Gary R. Bunt, *Islam in the Digital Age* (London: Pluto Press, 2003), 211.
41 Seib, *The Al Jazeera Effect*, 169–70.
42 Jon Alterman, "The Key Is Moving Beyond Spectacle," *Daily Star*, December 27, 2004.
43 Samantha M. Shapiro, "Ministering to the Upwardly Mobile Muslim," *New York Times Magazine*, April 30, 2006.
44 Linday Wise, "Amr Khaled vs. Yusuf Al Qaradawi: The Danish Cartoon Controversy and the Clash of Two Islamic TV Titans," *TBS Journal*, 16, June–December 2006.
45 McCants, "Militant Ideology Atlas," 9.
46 "Execution Footage a Dilemma for TV News," *Television Week*, January 8, 2007.

47 Brian Stelter and Noam Cohen, "Citizen Journalists Provide Glimpses into Attacks," *New York Times*, November 30, 2008.
48 Mark Mazzetti, "Jihad Ideology Is Spreading Online," *New York Times*, October 14, 2006.
49 United States Senate Committee on Homeland Security and Governmental Affairs, "Violent Islamist Extremism," 12–13.
50 Corman, Trethewey, and Goodall, *Weapons of Mass Persuasion*, 122–3.
51 Weimann, *Terror on the Internet*, 116.

2 High tech terror: Al Qaeda and beyond

1 "Winning or Losing: A Special Report on Al Qaeda," *Economist*, July 19, 2008, 4–5.
2 National Commission on Terrorist Attacks upon the United States, *The 9/11 Commission Report* (New York: W. W. Norton, 2004), 362.
3 See Marc Sageman, *Leaderless Jihad* (Philadelphia: University of Pennsylvania Press, 2008).
4 "Winning or Losing," 8–9.
5 Peter Bergen, "Reading Al Qaeda," *Washington Post*, September 11, 2005.
6 Bruce Riedel, "Al Qaeda Strikes Back," *Foreign Affairs*, 86, no. 3 (May/June 2007), 24.
7 "Winning or Losing," 12.
8 "The Growing, and Mysterious, Irrelevance of Al Qaeda," *Economist*, January 24, 2009, 64.
9 Steve Coll and Susan B. Glasser, "Terrorists Move Operations to Cyberspace," *Washington Post*, August 7, 2005.
10 Craig Whitlock, "Briton Used Internet as His Bully Pulpit," *Washington Post*, August 8, 2005.
11 Michael Scheuer, *Imperial Hubris* (Dulles, VA: Brassey's, 2004) 79, 81.
12 Douglas Frantz, Josh Meyer, and Richard B. Schmitt, "Cyberspace Gives Al Qaeda Refuge," *Los Angeles Times*, August 15, 2004.
13 Coll and Glasser, "Terrorists Move Operations to Cyberspace."
14 Coll and Glasser, "Terrorists Move Operations to Cyberspace."
15 Gabriel Weimann, *Terror on the Internet* (Washington, DC: United States Institute of Peace, 2006), 65, 67; "Al Qaeda Internet Magazine *Sawt al-Jihad* Calls to Intensify Fighting During Ramadan," Jihad Watch, www.jihadwatch.org/archives/003647
16 Weimann, *Terror on the Internet*, 66.
17 Peter Bergen, "Al Qaeda, Still in Business," *Washington Post*, July 2, 2006.
18 Craig Whitlock, "The New Al Qaeda Central," *Washington Post*, September 9, 2007.
19 Shaun Waterman, "Zawahiri Pledges Online Chat," United Press International, December 17, 2007; www.upi.com/international_security/emerging_threats/analysis/2007/12/17/analysis.
20 "Al Zawahiri in Two Recent Messages," Middle East Media Research Institute Special Dispatch Series no. 1787, December 18, 2007.
21 Faisal Devji, *Landscapes of the Jihad* (Ithaca, NY: Cornell University Press, 2005), 137.
22 Weimann, *Terror on the Internet*, 44.
23 Cited in Devji, *Landscapes of the Jihad*, 64.
24 Craig Whitlock, "Al Qaeda Masters Terrorism on the Cheap," *Washington Post*, August 24, 2008.
25 "Al Qaeda Second-in-Command Ayman Al-Zawahiri Threatens France, States Obama No Different than Bush," Middle East Media Research Institute Special Dispatch Series no. 2475, August 5, 2009.

26 Brynjar Lia, "Al Qaeda's Appeal: Understanding Its Unique Selling Points," *Perspectives on Terrorism*, II, no. 8, May 2008, 6.

27 Hanna Rogan, "Abu Reuter and the E-Jihad," *Georgetown Journal of International Affairs*, no. 8.2 (Summer/Fall 2007), 89.

28 Michael Scheuer, "Al Qaeda's Media Doctrine: Evolution from Cheerleader to Opinion-Shaper," *Jamestown Foundation Terrorism Focus*, 4, no. 15, May 22, 2007.

29 "As Sahab: Al Qaeda's Nebulous Media Branch," *Stratfor Daily Terrorism Brief*, September 8, 2006; Craig Whitlock, "Al Qaeda's Growing Online Offensive," *Washington Post*, June 24, 2008.

30 Whitlock, "Al Qaeda's Growing Online Offensive"; "As Sahab Posts," CBS News Internet Terror Monitor, www.cbsnews.com/sections/monitor/main502684.shtml? keyword=As+Sahab& tag=contentMain;contentBody

31 Peter Bergen, "Al Qaeda at 20, Dead or Alive?", *Washington Post*, August 17, 2008.

32 "Greyhawk," "Al Qaeda's 'Working Paper for a Media Invasion of America,'" www.mudvillegazette.com/archives/006694.html

33 Andrew Black, "Al Qaeda in the Maghreb's Burgeoning Media Apparatus," *Jamestown Foundation Terrorism Focus*, V, no. 14, May 15, 2007.

34 "Jihad and Terrorism Threat Monitor Weekly Digest," no. 9, December 17–24, 2009, MEMRI (e-mail).

35 Whitlock, "Al Qaeda's Growing Online Offensive."

36 Hanna Rogan, "Jihadism Online," Forsvarets Forskninginstitutt, Norwegian Defense Research Establishment, FFI/Rapport 2006/00915, March 2006.

37 Anne Stenersen, "The Internet: A Virtual Training Camp?" *Terrorism and Political Violence*, 20 (2008), 216.

38 Stenersen, "The Internet: A Virtual Training Camp?" 216.

39 Brymjar Lia, "Al Qaeda Online: Understanding Jihadist Internet Infrastructure," *Jane's Intelligence Review*, January 1, 2006; Stenersen, "The Internet: A Virtual Training Camp?" 219.

40 Stenersen, "The Internet: A Virtual Training Camp?" 222, 227.

41 "New Jihad Magazine Targets Western Audience," Anti-Defamation League, August 3, 2009. www.adl.org/main_Terrorism/default.htm

42 Michael Moss and Souad Mekhennet, "An Internet Jihad Aims at U.S. Viewers," *New York Times*, October 15, 2007.

43 Susan B. Glasser and Steve Coll, "The Web as Weapon," *Washington Post*, August 9, 2005.

44 Nadya Labi. "Jihad 2.0," *Atlantic Monthly*, July-August 2006, 102.

45 Marc Lynch, "Al Qaeda's Media Strategies," *National Interest*, Spring 2006.

46 Scott Shane, "Zarqawi Built Global Jihadist Network on Internet," *New York Times*, June 9, 2006.

47 Daniel Byman, *The Five Front War* (New York: Wiley, 2008), 227.

48 Lia, "Al Qaeda Online."

49 Rogan, "Abu Reuter and the E-Jihad," 93.

50 Y. Yehoshua, "Islamist Websites as an Integral Part of Jihad: A General Overview," MEMRI Jihad and Terrorism Studies Project, no. 328, February 21, 2007.

51 Lia, "Al Qaeda Online."

52 Abdul Hameed Bakier, "Jihadis Publish Online Recruitment Manual," *Jamestown Foundation Terrorism Focus*, 5, no. 34, September 24, 2008.

53 Labi, "Jihad 2.0," 103; Abdul Hameed Bakier, "Watching the Watchers: A Jihadi View of Terrorism Analysis Websites," *Jamestown Foundation Terrorism Focus*, 5, no. 33, September 18, 2008.

54 Scott Shane, "Born in U.S., a Radical Cleric Inspires Terror," *New York Times*, November 19, 2009.

55 Abdul Hameed Bakier, "Jihadis Search for Security Presence on Jihadi Website Forums," *Jamestown Foundation Terrorism Monitor*, 7, no. 25, August 13, 2009.

56 "Your First Step To Circumvent Electronic Transactions," NEFA Foundation, April 7, 2009, www.nefafoundation.org/miscellaneous/featureddocs/nefafinancejihad sites0409
57 Weimann, *Terror on the Internet*, 115.
58 Shane, "Born in U.S., a Radical Cleric Inspires Terror."
59 International Crisis Group, "Taliban Propaganda: Winning the War of Words?" *Asia Report* no. 158, July 24, 2008, 14.
60 International Crisis Goup, "Taliban Propaganda," 15–16.
61 Ed Blanche, "Islam's Secret Army?" *The Middle East*, August/September 2008, 17, 19.
62 Zeyno Baran, "Fighting the War of Ideas," *Foreign Affairs*, 84, no. 6 (November/December 2005), 72–3.
63 FARC material research assistance and translation provided by Daniela Montiel.
64 www.youtube.com/watch?v=ug4TvhzReqc
65 www.youtube.com/watch?v=SoP3O5plQxU& feature=related
66 Christina Neumayer and Celina Raffl, "Facebook for Protest? The Value of Social Software for Political Activism in the Anti-FARC Rallies," DigiActive Research Series, December 2008, 1–2, www.scribd.com/doc/1735224q; Juan Forero and Karin Brulliard, "Anti-FARC Rallies Held Worldwide," *Washington Post*, February 5, 2008.
67 Neumayer and Raffl, "Facebook for Protest?" 6; Sibylla Brodzinsky, "Internet Site to Spawn Protests in 185 Cities Monday Against Rebel Group's Methods," *Christian Science Monitor*, February 4, 2008.
68 ELN material research assistance and translation provided by Daniela Montiel.
69 www.cfr.org/publication/9272/
70 www.youtube.com/watch?v=vS-FxjbDKU4& feature=player_embedded
71 Merlyna Lim, *Islamic Radicalism and Anti-Americanism in Indonesia: The Role of the Internet* (Washington, DC: East-West Center, 2005), 18.
72 Evan F. Kohlmann, "Prominent Jihad Media Organizations in Central Asia," NEFA Foundation, March 2009, www.nefafounddation.org/miscellaneous/feature ddocs/nefajihadmedia0309

3 Terrorists' online strategies

1 Hussein Ibish and Anne Stewart, *Report on Hate Crimes and Discrimination Against Arab-Americans: The Post September 11 Back-lash* (American-Arab Anti-Discrimination Committee, 2003), www.adc.org/PDF/hcr02.pdf
2 Cynthia Dizikes, "Muslim Families Removed from AirTran Flight Get Apology," *LA Times*, January 3, 2009, http://articles.latimes.com/2009/jan/03/nation/na-muslim-passengers3
3 Pew Research Center, *Views of Religious Similarities and Differences* (2009), http://people-press.org/reports/pdf/542.pdf
4 U.S. Department of State Office of the Coordinator for Counterterrorism, "Foreign Terrorist Organizations," December 30, 2009, www.state.gov/s/ct/rls/other/des/123085.htm
5 Alex P. Schmid and Janny de Graaf, *Violence as Communication: Insurgent Terrorism and the Western News Media* (Beverly Hills, CA: Sage Publications, 1982).
6 Michael Whine, "Cyberspace—A New Medium for Communication, Command, and Control by Extremists," *Studies in Conflict and Terrorism*, 22 (1999), 231–245.
7 Paul Wolfowitz, *Prepared Statement for the House Armed Services Committee* (Washington, DC: August 10, 2004), www.defenselink.mil/speeches/speech.aspx?speechid=143
8 Jenine Abboushi Dallal, "Hizballah's Virtual Civil Society," *Television and New Media*, no. 4 (2001), 367–72.

9 Jon Swartz, "Terrorists' Use of Internet Spreads," *USA Today*, February 21, 2005, www.usatoday.com/money/industries/technology/2005-02-20-cyber-terror-usat_x.htm

10 Gabriel Weimann, "Virtual disputes: The Use of the Internet for Terrorist Debates," *Studies in Conflicts and Terrorism*, 7 (2006), 623–39.

11 Gabriel Weimann, *Terror on the Internet: The New Trends*, Speech delivered at the University of Miami School of Communication, Coral Gables, FL, October 23, 2008.

12 John Arquilla, David Ronfeldt, and Michele Zanini, "Globally Wired: Politics in Cyberspace (fourth in a series): Information-Age Terrorism," *Current History*, 99, no. 636 (2000), 179–85.

13 Bruce Hoffman, *The Use of the Internet by Islamic Extremists*, Testimony presented to the House Permanent Select Committee on Intelligence, May, 2006, 5.

14 Holsti's elements are an adaptation of the work of Alfred R. Lindesmith in 1931.

15 Hamza Aktan, "Acts of Terror and Suicide Attacks in the Light of the Qur'an and the Sunna," in Ergün Çapan (ed.), *Terror and Suicide Attacks: An Islamic Perspective* (New Jersey, NJ: The Light, 2005), 27.

16 Ibrahim Canan, "Islam as the Religion of Peace and Tolerance," in Ergün Çapan (ed.), *Terror and Suicide Attacks: An Islamic Perspective* (New Jersey, NJ: The Light, 2005), 9–24.

17 As cited in Nuriye Akman, "Interview with M. Fethullah Gülen," in Ergün Çapan (ed.), *Terror and Suicide Attacks: An Islamic Perspective* (New Jersey, NJ: The Light, 2005), 2–8.

18 Bekir Karlığa, "Religion, Terror, War, and the Need for Global Ethics," in Ergün Çapan (ed.), *Terror and Suicide Attacks: An Islamic Perspective* (New Jersey, NJ: The Light, 2005), 44–62.

19 Ali Bulaç, "Jihad," in Ergün Çapan (ed.), *Terror and Suicide Attacks: An Islamic Perspective* (New Jersey, NJ: The Light, 2005), 63–78.

20 Assaf Moghadam, "Defining Suicide Terrorism," in Ami Pedahzur (ed.), *Root Causes of Suicide Terrorism: The Globalization of Martyrdom* (New York, NY: Routledge, 2006).

21 Gilles Kepel, *The War for Muslim Minds: Islam and the West* (Cambridge, MA: The Belknap Press of Harvard University Press, 2004).

22 Moghadam, "Defining Suicide Terrorism."

23 Hoffman, "Use of the Internet by Islamic Extremists."

24 Fred Cohen, "Terrorism and Cyberspace," *Network Security* (2002), 17–19; Steven Furnell and Mathew Warren, "Computer Hacking and Cyberterrorism: The Real Threats in the New Millennium," *Computers and Society*, no. 1 (1999), 28–34; Timothy L. Thomas, "Al Qaeda and the Internet: The Danger of 'Cyberplanning,'" *Parameters*, 33, no. 1 (2003), 112–23; Gabriel Weimann, *www.terror.net: How Modern Terrorism Uses the Internet* (Washington, DC: United States Institute of Peace, 2004, 1), www.usip.org/pubs/specialreports/sr116.pdf

25 Fernando Reinares, "Who are the Terrorists? Analyzing Changes in Sociological Profile among Members of ETA," *Studies in Conflict and Terrorism*, 27, no. 6, (2004), 465–88.

26 Charles Russell and Bowman Miller, "Profile of a Terrorist," *Terrorism: An International Journal*, 1, no. 1 (1977), 17–34.

27 Dallal, "Hizballah's Virtual Civil Society."

28 Paul Eedle and Huda Ali (producer). *Jihad TV: Terrorism and Mass Media* [Motion picture], (USA: Films for the Humanities and Sciences, 2006).

29 Ibid.

30 Ibid.

31 Ibid.

32 Evan F. Kohlmann, "The Real Online Terrorist Threat," *Foreign Affairs*, 85, no. 5 (2006), 115–124.

33 Eedle and Ali, *Jihad TV.*
34 Thomas, "Al Qaeda and the Internet."
35 Marc Sageman, *Leaderless Jihad: Terror Networks in the Twenty-First Century* (Philadelphia, PA: University of Pennsylvania Press, 2008).
36 Cohen, "Terrorism and Cyberspace"; Furnell and Warren, "Computer Hacking and Cyberterrorism";Thomas, "Al Qaeda and the Internet"; Weimann, *www.terror.net.*
37 Cohen, "Terrorism and Cyberspace"; Weimann, *www.terror.net.*
38 Barbara Berman, "Remarks by Barbara Berman," in *Combating Terrorist Uses of the Internet.* Proceedings of the American Society of International Law Annual Meeting, 2005, 104–8; Furnell and Warren, "Computer Hacking and Cyberterrorism"; Thomas, "Al Qaeda and the Internet."
39 Cohen, "Terrorism and Cyberspace"; Furnell and Warren, "Computer Hacking and Cyberterrorism"; Thomas, "Al Qaeda and the Internet"; Weimann, *www.terror.net.*
40 Berman, "Remarks by Barbara Berman"; Thomas, "Al Qaeda and the Internet"; Weimann, *www.terror.net.*
41 Thomas Steinfatt, "Propaganda Theory," in Stephen W. Littlejohn and Karen A. Foss (eds.), *Encyclopedia of Communication Theory* (Thousand Oaks, CA: Sage, 2010).
42 Jeremy Kahn, "Mumbai Terrorists Relied on New Technology for Attacks," *New York Times*, December 9, 2008, www.nytimes.com/2008/12/09/world/asia/09mumbai.html?pagewanted=print
43 Raymond Bonner, "A Terror Strike, Choreographed on a Computer," *New York Times*, July 3, 2006, www.nytimes.com/2006/07/03/world/asia/03bali.html?scp=21& sq=terror%20internet& st=cse#
44 "Al Qaeda Spreads Jihad via the Internet," *Pravda*, October 8, 2005.
45 Susan Stellin, "Terror's Confounding Online Trail," *New York Times*, March 28, 2002, http://query.nytimes.com/gst/fullpage.html?res=9D07EFD8103BF93BA15750C0 A9649C8B63& scp=16& sq=terror%20internet& st=cse
46 Weimann, *www.terror.net.*
47 James Risen and David Johnston, "A Nation Challenged: The Terrorist; Al Qaeda May be Rebuilding in Pakistan, E-mails Indicate," *New York Times*, March 6, 2002, http://query.nytimes.com/gst/fullpage.html?res=9C04EFD71230F935A35750 C0A9649C8B63& scp=17& sq=terror%20internet& st=cse#
48 "Sympathizers Seek Answers from Al-Qaida: Questions to al-Zawahri for 'On-line Interview' Unanswered So Far," *The Associated Press*, January 21, 2008, www. msnbc.msn.com/id/22767244/from/ET/
49 Thomas, "Al Qaeda and the Internet."
50 Swartz, "Terrorists' Use of Internet Spreads."
51 Ibid., para. 15.
52 Thomas, "Al Qaeda and the Internet."
53 Jialun Qin, Yilu Zhou, Edna Reid, Guanpi Lai, and Hsinchun Chen, "Analyzing Terror Campaigns on the Internet: Technical Sophistication, Content Richness, and Web Interactivity," *International Journal of Human Computer Studies*, 65, no. 1 (2007), 83.
54 Yariv Tsfati and Gabriel Weimann, "www.terrorism.com: Terror on the Internet," *Studies in Conflict and Terrorism*, 25, no. 5 (2002), 317–32.
55 Dallal, "Hizballah's Virtual Civil Society."
56 Bruce Hoffman, "Use of the Internet by Islamic Extremists," Testimony presented to the House Permanent Select Committee on Intelligence, May, 2006.
57 Weimann, *www.terror.net.*
58 Ibid.
59 Dallal, "Hizballah's Virtual Civil Society."
60 Tsfati and Weimann, "www.terrorism.com."

61 Berman, "Remarks by Barbara Berman."
62 Patrick Radden Keefe, "Exposing the 'Darknet': Are al Qaeda Terrorists Using your Personal Computer?" *Village Voice*, February 8, 2005, www.villagevoice.com/news/0507,essay,61085,2.html
63 Berman, "Remarks by Barbara Berman."
64 Richard Kahn and Douglas Kellner, "New Media and Internet Activism: From the 'Battle of Seattle' to Blogging," *New Media and Society*, 6, no. 1 (2004), 87–95.
65 Keefe, "Exposing the 'Darknet.'"
66 Peter Biddle, Paul England, Marcus Peinado, and Bryan Willman, "The Darknet and the Future of Content Distribution," *Lecture Notes in Computer Science*, 2696 (2003), 155–76.
67 Weimann, *www.terror.net*.
68 Berman, "Remarks by Barbara Berman."
69 Steve Coll and Susan B. Glasser, "Terrorists Turn to the Web as Base of Operations," *Washington Post*, August 7, 2005, 1.
70 Al Boraq Media Organization, *Islamic Army in Iraq*, http://iaisite-eng.org/
71 Coll and Glasser, "Terrorists Turn to the Web as Base of Operations."
72 Hoffman, "Use of the Internet by Islamic Extremists."
73 Michael Y. Dartnell, *Insurgency Online: Web Activism and Global Conflict* (Toronto, Canada: University of Toronto Press, 2006), 19.
74 Arquilla, Ronfeldt, and Zanini, "Globally Wired," 180.
75 Dartnell, *Insurgency Online*, 28.
76 Miniwatts Marketing Group, *Internet Usage Statistics* (2009), www.internetworldstats.com/stats.htm
77 Daniel Kimmage, "Fight Terror with YouTube," *New York Times*, June 26, 2008, www.nytimes.com/2008/06/26/opinion/26kimmage.html?scp=23&sq=terror%20internet&st=cse
78 Sageman, *Leaderless Jihad*.
79 Kimmage, "Fight Terror with YouTube."
80 James A. Lewis, "The Internet and Terrorism," in Ashley Deeks, Barbara Berman, Susan Brenner, and James A. Lewis, *Combating Terrorist Uses of the Internet* (Proceedings of the American Society of International Law Annual Meeting, 2005), 113.
81 Hoffman, "Use of the Internet by Islamic Extremists," 16.
82 Coll and Glasser, "Terrorists Turn to the Web as Base of Operations."
83 Michele Zanini and Sean J. A. Edwards, "The Networking of Terror in the Information Age," in John Arquilla and David Ronfeldt (eds.), *Networks and Netwars: The Future of Terror, Crime and Militancy* (Arlington, VA: RAND Corporation, 2001), 39.
84 Thomas, "Al Qaeda and the Internet," 115.
85 Eedle and Ali, *Jihad TV*.
86 Maura Conway, "Terrorism and the Internet," *Parliamentary Affairs*, 59, no. 2 (2006), 296.

4 Targeting the young

1 Peter W. Singer, "Terrorists Must Be Denied Child Recruits," *Financial Times*, January 20, 2005.
2 "Participation of Children and Teenagers in Terrorist Activity During the Al-Aqsa Intifada," Israel Ministry of Foreign Affairs, January 30, 2003, www.mfa.gov.il
3 "Cubs of Al-Qaeda in the Islamic Maghreb [Morocco]." N.d. Retrieved December 16, 2009, from www.youtube.com/watch?v=Or8foRylt8Y
4 "Iraq Dismantles 'Lion Cubs' Terrorist Cell," *Trend*, August 5, 2009, en.trend.az/print/1517548.html

5 http://web.worldbank.org/WBSITE/EXTERNAL/DATASTATISTICS/0,contentMDK:20394859~menuPK:1192714~

6 U.S. Senate Committee on Homeland Security and Governmental Affairs, "Violent Islamist Extremism," 13.

7 www.facebook.com/press/info.php?statistics

8 Manav Tanneeru, "Young Muslims Turn to Technology to connect, Challenge Traditions," CNN.com, www.cnn.com/2009/WORLD/meast/08/07generationislam. tech/index.html, accessed August 7, 2009.

9 www.mecca.com/aboutus, accessed August 9, 2009.

10 www.mideastyouth.com/about-us and www.mideastyouth.com/faq, accessed August 9, 2009.

11 Tanneeru, "Young Muslims Turn."

12 Castells, *The Power of Identity*, 69.

13 "A Present from Daddy: Machine Gun and Rifle." February 26, 2006. Palestinian Authority TV. Retrieved December 16, 2009, from www.youtube.com/watch? v=pF1uFTB4_hs& NR=1.

14 "Palestinian Child Vows to Avenge Death of Terrorist Father," August 23, 2002. Palestinian Authority TV. Retrieved December 16, 2009, from www.youtube.com/ watch?v=IOSX44kZi3M& feature=related.

15 "Children in the Service of Terror," Middle East Media Research Institute, Special Dispatch 2455, July 21, 2009.

16 Alan Travis, "The Making of an Extremist," *Guardian*, August 20, 2008.

17 "UK: Children Involved in Terrorism," CNN.com, http://edition.cnn.com/2007/ world/europe/11/05/britain.threat/index

18 Tara Bahrampour, "Muslim Leaders Look Inward After Arrests of N. Va. Men," *Washington Post*, December 25, 2009.

19 Mark Hughes, "Police Identify 200 Children as Potential Terrorists," *Independent*, March 28, 2009.

20 Singer, "Terrorists Must Be Denied Child Recruits."

21 "Participation of Children and Teenagers."

22 See, for example, www.mideastweb.org/educdir

23 "Inside the New Hezbollah Video Game: 'Special Force 2'," *Asharq Al-Awsat*, August 20, 2007; "Hezbollah Video Game: War with Israel," CNN.com, www.cnn. com/2007/world/meast/08/16/hezbollah.game.reut

24 www.peacemakergame.com

25 www.americasarmy.com

26 www.youtube.com/watch?v=J-FVCIBRmOE.

27 Weimann, *Terror on the Internet*, 91.

28 Craig S. Smith, "Warm and Fuzzy TV, Brought to You by Hamas," *New York Times*, January 18, 2006; Seib, *The Al Jazeera Effect*, 28.

29 Middle East Media Research Institute, Special Dispatch Series no. 1577 (May 9, 2007), no. 1657 (July 16, 2007), no. 1683 (August 17, 2007); www.memri.org

30 "Hamas TV Bunny Assud Killed," MEMRI Special Dispatch 2228, February 4, 2009.

31 "Hamas puppet: I Declare War on the Zionists," MEMRI Palestinian Media Watch, February 15, 2009.

32 "New Animated Film on Hamas TV Focuses on Child Martyrdom," MEMRI Special Dispatch 1742, October 16, 2007.

33 Vivian Salama, "Hamas TV: Palestinian Media in Transition," *Transnational Broadcasting Studies Journal*, no. 16, June-December 2006; Seib, *The Al Jazeera Effect*, 27.

34 "Anti-Semitism on Egypt's Al-Rahma TV," MEMRI Special Dispatch 2466, July 30, 2009.

35 www.awladnaa.net/madena.php?ID_subject=50& do=show& cat=7; www.awladnaa. net/medena.php?ID_subject=223& do=show& cat=5; both accessed April 17, 2006.

36 MEMRI Special Dispatch 1018 and www.memritv.org/search.asp?ACT=S9& P1=906, accessed November 2, 2005.
37 "Saudi Columnist: How to Keep Your Son from Becoming a Terrorist," MEMRI Special Dispatch 2241, February 12, 2009.

5 Women and terrorism

1 Barbara Victor, *Army of Roses: Inside the World of Palestinian Women Suicide Bombers* (New York: St. Martin's Press, 2003).
2 Robert Pape, *Dying to Win: The Strategic Logic of Suicide Terrorism* (New York: Random House, 2005).
3 Rosemarie Skaine, *Female Suicide Bombers* (Jefferson, NC: McFarland & Company, 2006).
4 "Female Suicide Bomber Strikes Football Fans," *Jordan Times*, June 15, 2008, http://jordantimes.com/index.php?news=8614& searchFor=female suicide
5 "The Enemies of Jealousy and Honor," *Islamic Army in Iraq*, October 8, 2009, www.iaisite.net/
6 "The Deployment of Women Police Officers to the Streets of Nablus," *Al-Quds*, January 21, 2009. http://web.alquds.com/node/132113
7 "Women Police start their Work in Nablus," *Saraya Al-Quds*, 2008, http://forum.saraya.ps/showthread.php?t=7568
8 Noora Younis, "'Al-Masry Al-Youm' Reveals Pictures: Palestinian Women Join the 'Heart' of the Resistance," *Al-Masry Al-Youm*, March 16, 2009, www.almasry-alyoum.com/article2.aspx?ArticleID=203046& IssueID=1346
9 "Mojahidat Saraya Al-Quds," *InfoLive TV*, 2008, www.youtube.com/watch?v=z80a-aApsjc& feature=fvw
10 InfoLive TV, www.infolive.tv/en/home
11 "Israel Union Drops Exhibit Portraying Terrorists as Virgin Mary," *Haaretz*, September 3, 3009, www.haaretz.com/hasen/spages/1112232.html
12 "Al Qaeda Female Bombers Signal Despair—Analysts," *Jordan Times*, January 6, 2008, http://jordantimes.com/index.php?news=4774& searchFor=female suicide
13 Amira Abd Al-Rahman, "University Graduates, Mothers, and Women with Infants Sacrifice Themselves for the Sake of the [Palestinian] Cause," *Al-Masry Al-Youm*, March 16, 2009, www.almasry-alyoum.com/article2.aspx?ArticleID=203049& IssueID=1346
14 "Palestinian Women are a Strategic Stockpile for the Resistance," *IslamWeb*, October 18, 2009, www.islamweb.net/media/index.php?page=article& lang=A& id=74779
15 "The Palestinian Women Have the Credit to Take a Nobel Prize in Resisting the Aggression," *Ezzedeen Al-Qassam Brigades: Information Office*, 2006, www.qassam.ps/news-218-The_Palestinian_women_have_the_credit_to_take_A_Nobel_Prize_in_Resisting_the_aggression.html
16 "Reem Rayasi Farewell Hamas Website," *YouTube*, www.youtube.com/watch?v=uRDuKzC23GI
17 "One Year After the Summer War—Sixth Episode: Women of Hizballah," *Asharq Al-Awsat*, July 17, 2007, www.aawsat.com/details.asp?issueno=10458& article=428464
18 "Letter of Mojahid to His Mother," *Al-Qassam English Forum*, October 31, 2009, www.almoltaqa.ps/english/showthread.php?t=13683
19 *Al-Rafedean News Network*, http://alrafdean.org/node/106651
20 "Mission Statement: The Women's Movement Against the Occupation and Domination," *The Nationalist and Islamic Front*, March 6, 2008, www.jabha-wqs.net/article.php?id=371
21 *Turn to Islam Forum*, www.turntoislam.com/forum/index.php
22 *Eye on Palestine Forum*, www.iopal.net/forum/
23 *Islamic View*, http://islam.trivuz.com/forums/showthread.php?tid=334

24 *Mahjoob.com*, www.mahjoob.com/en/forums/showthread.php?t=249815
25 "Gama'a al-Islamiyya: Family Matters," *Al-Jamaa Al-Islamiya*, www.egyig.com/archive.php?type=family& id=44
26 "The Palestinian Women Have the Credit to Take a Nobel Prize in Resisting the Aggression."
27 "Muslim Family Forum," *Al-Boraq*, http://alboraq.info/forumdisplay.php?f=92
28 "Opening of the First Woman to Design a Mosque," *Al-Qassam English Forum*, August 1, 2009, www.almoltaqa.ps/english/showthread.php?t=12550
29 *The Army of Saad bin abi Waqas*, http://saadarmy.com/jm159/index.php?option=com_content& view=category& id=39& Itemid=100
30 "Muslim Family Matters: The Role of Muslim Woman in Jihad," *Al-Boraq*, September 2009, http://alboraq.info/showthread.php?t=137727
31 "One Year After the Summer War—Sixth Episode: Women of Hizballah."
32 "The Wife of Al-Zawahiri: The Battle for the Veil is One the Most Difficult," *Asharq Al-Awsat*, December 18, 2009, www.aawsat.com/details.asp?section=4& issueno=11343& article=549064
33 "Palestinian Female Martyrs," *Yards of Arab Aviation*, October 1, 2009, http://4flying.com/showthread.php?t=35759
34 "Women of Resistance from Gaza," *A Touch of Love: A Woman's Forum*, January 25, 2009, http://vb.lamst7b.net/l16531/
35 *Keyboard TK*, www.klavyem.tk/filistinli-kiz-israil-sinir-gorevlisini-bicakladi-izle.html
36 "The Role of Women in Jihad and Defending the Homeland," *Al-Boraq*, February 5, 2009, http://alboraq.info/showthread.php?t=89529
37 Karla Cunningham, "Cross Regional Trends in Female Terrorism," in Gus Martin (ed.), *The New Era of Terrorism: Selected Readings* (Thousand Oaks, CA: Sage, 2004).
38 "Jihad Is Worship," *Islamic Army in Iraq*, October 8, 2008, www.iaisite.net/

6 Terrorism's online future

1 Scott McConnell, "Foreign Occupation Is the Primary Cause of Suicide Terrorism," in Jacqueline Langwith (ed.), *Suicide* (Farmington Hills, MI: Greenhaven Press, 2008), 117.
2 E. F. Bruner, "U.S. Military Dispositions: Fact Sheet." *CSR report for Congress*, January 30, 2007, 1, www.fas.org/sgp/crs/natsec/RS20649.pdf
3 Hanna Rogan, "Abu Reuter and the E-Jihad," *Georgetown Journal of International Affairs*, 8.2 (Summer/Fall 2007), 89.
4 "Who is Anwar al-Awlaki?" *The Week*, January 4, 2009, www.theweek.com/article/index/102685/Who_is_Anwar_alAwlaki
5 Mark Hosenball, Michael Isikoff, and Evan Thomas, "The Radicalization of Umar Farouk Abdulmutallab," *Newsweek*, January 2, 2010, www.newsweek.com/id/229047
6 "Umar Farouk Abdulmutallab: One Boy's Journey to Jihad," *TimesOnline*, January 3, 2010, www.timesonline.co.uk/tol/news/world/middle_east/article6974073.ece
7 Daniel Martin Katz, Michael Bommarito, and Jonathan Zelner, "Visualizing the Gawaher Interactions of Umar Farouk Abdulmutallab, the Christmas Day Bomber," *Computational Legal Studies*, January 6, 2010, http://computationallegalstudies.com/2010/01/06/the-time-evolving-structure-of-the-gawaher-islamic-forum-as-experienced-by-umar-farouk-abdulmutallab-the-christmas-day-bomber/
8 Katz, Bommarito, and Zelner, "Visualizing the Gawaher Interactions of Umar Farouk Abdulmutallab, the Christmas Day Bomber."
9 Paul Hamilos, "The Worst Islamist Attack in European History," *Guardian*, October 31, 2007, www.guardian.co.uk/world/2007/oct/31/spain
10 Mitchell D. Silber and Arvin Bhatt, "Radicalization in the West: The Homegrown Threat," *The New York Police Department Intelligence Division*, 2007, www.nypdshield.org/public/SiteFiles/documents/NYPD_Report-Radicalization_in_the_West.pdf

11 Joseph Lieberman and Susan Collins, "Violent Islamist Extremism, the Internet, and the Homegrown Terrorist Threat," United States Senate Committee on Homeland Security and Governmental Affairs, May 8, 2008, 11, http://hsgac.senate.gov/public/_files/IslamistReport.pdf

12 Lieberman and Collins, "Violent Islamist Extremism, the Internet, and the Homegrown Terrorist Threat," 12.

13 Al-Qassam English Forum Rules, www.almoltaqa.ps/english/register.php

14 Al-Qassam English Forum, www.almoltaqa.ps/english/showthread.php?t=14048

15 Samir Al-Awrki, "Lessons from Al-Daawa: Al-Jamaa Al-Islamiya and Al-Qaeda," *Al-Jamaa Al-Islamiya*, www.egyig.com/Public/articles/scholars/11/59667515.shtml

16 Facebook Press Room, 2010, www.facebook.com/press/info.php?statistics

17 Michal Zippori and Kevin Flower, "Israel Warns Citizens to Beware of Facebook Spy Requests," CNN International, May 18, 2009, http://edition.cnn.com/2009/WORLD/meast/05/18/israel.facebook.spies/index.html?iref=mpstoryview

18 "Hezbollah Using Facebook to Kidnap Israeli Soldiers," *Ya Libnan*, September 7, 2008, http://yalibnan.com/site/archives/2008/09/hezbollah_using.php

19 Rachel Geizhals, "Social Media Users Successfully Face Down Nasrallah on Facebook," *The Jerusalem Post*, July 29, 2009, para. 3, www.jpost.com/servlet/Satellite?cid=1248277915968& pagename=JPArticle%2FShowFull

20 Miles Johnson, "British Students Being Recruited to Jihadist Facebook Groups," *The Journal*, February 15, 2008, para. 7, www.journal-online.co.uk/article/2849-british-students-being-recruited-to-jihadist-facebook-groups

21 Ally Fogg, "Twitter Terrorist Arrest: Cause for Concern," *Guardian*, January 18, 2010, www.guardian.co.uk/commentisfree/libertycentral/2010/jan/18/twitter-terror-arrest

22 304 Military Intelligence Battalion Open Source Intelligence Team (Ml Bn OSINT Team), "alQaida-Like Mobile Discussions and Potential Creative Uses," *The Federation of American Scientists*, October 16, 2008, 1–2, www.fas.org/irp/eprint/mobile.pdf

23 "Obama Says Bin Laden Tape Shows al-Qaeda 'Weakened,'" BBC News, January 26, 2010, http://news.bbc.co.uk/2/hi/americas/8481079.stm

24 Inshallahshaheed: The Ignored Puzzle Pieces of Knowledge, http://revolution.ansar1.net/

25 Society for Internet Research, www.sofir.org/

26 "Blogs Target Jihadis Online," *Washington Times*, October 10, 2007, www.washingtontimes.com/news/2007/oct/10/blogs-target-jihadis-online/

27 Michael Moss and Souad Mekhennet, "An Internet Jihad Aims at U.S. Viewers," *New York Times*, October 17, 2008, www.nytimes.com/2007/10/15/us/15net.html?_r=1&oref=slogin

28 Ibid., para. 7.

29 Al-Qassam English Forum, www.almoltaqa.ps/english/showthread.php?t=13655

30 Jerusalem Jihadi Forums, www.al-amanh.net/vb/showthread.php?t=1671

31 Alissa J. Rubin, "Taliban Overhaul Image to Win Allies," *New York Times*, January 21, 2010, paras. 4, 8. www.nytimes.com/2010/01/21/world/asia/21taliban.html?scp=1& sq=taliban%20overhaul%20image& st=cse

32 Lieberman and Collins, "Violent Islamist Extremism, the Internet, and the Homegrown Terrorist Threat," 8.

7 Responding to terrorism

1 Bruce Riedel, "Al Qaeda Strikes Back," *Foreign Affairs*, 86, no. 3 (May/June 2007), 31.

2 David Kilcullen, *The Accidental Guerrilla: Fighting Small Wars in the Midst of a Big One* (New York: Oxford University Press, 2009), 281.

3 Daniel Silverberg and Joseph Heimann, "An Ever-Expanding War: Legal Aspects of Online Strategic Communication," *Parameters*, 39, no. 2 (Summer 2009), 77.
4 Scott Atran, "To Beat Al Qaeda, Look to the East," *New York Times*, December 13, 2009.
5 Silverberg and Heimann, "An Ever-Expanding War," 78.
6 Kilcullen, *The Accidental Guerrilla*, 300.
7 "9/11 Brings Mayhem to Jihadi Internet," MEMRI Special Dispatch 2530, September 11, 2009.
8 Kim Hart, "A New Breed of Hackers Tracks Online Acts of War," *Washington Post*, August 27, 2008.
9 Andrew Gray, "Pentagon Approves Creation of Cyber Command," Reuters, June 23, 2009.
10 Siobhan Gorman, Yochi J. Dreazen, and August Cole, "Insurgents Hack U.S. Drones," *Wall Street Journal*, December 17, 2009.
11 Thomas L. Friedman, "America vs. 'The Narrative,'" *New York Times*, November 29, 2009.
12 John Kifner, "Massacre Draws Self-Criticism in Muslim Press," *New York Times*, September 9, 2004.
13 Jessica Stern, "Mind Over Martyr," *Foreign Affairs*, 89, no. 1 (January/February 2010), 97.
14 "The Battle for a Religion's Heart," *Economist*, August 8, 2009, 52.
15 Juliana Menasce Horowitz, "Declining Support for bin Laden and Suicide Bombing," Pew Global Attitude Project, September 10, 2009, pewresearch.org/pubs/1338/declining-muslim-support-for-bin-laden-suicide-bombing
16 Council on Foreign Relations, ""Public Opinion on Global Issues," November 2009, www.cfr.org/public_opinion
17 Christopher Boucek, "The Sakinah Campaign and Internet Counter-Radicalization in Saudi Arabia," *CTC Sentinel* (Combating Terrorism Center), 1, no. 9 (August 2008), 3.
18 Y. Yehoshua, "Reeducation of Extremists in Saudi Arabia," MEMRI Inquiry and Analysis Series Report no. 260, January 18, 2006, www.memri.org/report/en/0/0/0/0/0/0/1582.htm
19 "Global Jihad—Opposition and Dissent," *Jihad and Terrorism Monitor Weekly Digest*, MEMRI, Special Dispatch 2676, December 4, 2009.
20 Reuel Marc Gerecht, "Speaking Truth to Muslim Power," *Wall Street Journal*, April 16, 2009.
21 Bernard Lewis, "Free at Last? The Arab World in the Twenty-first Century," *Foreign Affairs*, 88, no. 2 (March/April 2009), 87.
22 Rashad Hussain and al-Husein N. Madhany, "Reformulating the Battle of Ideas: Understanding the Role of Islam in Counterterrorism Policy," The Brookings Project on U.S. Relations with the Islamic World, Saban Center, The Brookings Institution, Analysis Paper no. 13, August 2008, 9.
23 Hussain and Madhany, "Reformulating the Battle of Ideas," 12.
24 Jarret Brachman, Brian Fishman, and Joseph Felter, "The Power of Truth: Questions for Ayman al-Zawahiri," Combating Terrorism Center, United States Military Academy, April 21, 2008.
25 Daniel Kimmage, "Fight Terror with YouTube," *New York Times*, June 26, 2008.
26 Alan Travis, "Revealed: Britain's Secret Propaganda War Against Al Qaeda," *Guardian*, August 26, 2008.
27 Alan Travis, "Battle against Al Qaeda Brand Highlighted in Secret Paper," *Guardian*, August 26, 2008.
28 Robert M. Gates, Landon Lecture, Kansas State University, November 26, 2007, www.defense.gov/speeches/speech.aspx?speechid=1199.
29 www.mideastyouth.com/projects; www.march18.org

30 international.daralhayat.com/internationalarticle/44327
31 "The Return of the Nativists," *Economist*, December 5, 2009, 71.
32 Samantha M. Shapiro, "Can the Muppets Make Friends in Ramallah?" *New York Times Magazine*, October 4, 2009; "Shara'a Simsim Spreads Hope and Empowerment to Palestinian Children," Sesame Workshop, www.sesameworkshop.org/aroundtheworld/palestine; Jen Christensen, "Reaching the Next Generation with 'Muppet Diplomacy,'" August 13, 2009, www.cnn.com/2009/world/meast/08/13/generation.islam.gaza.muppets/index
33 "Rruga Sesam/Ulica Sezam Humanizes the 'Other' in a Recovering Region," Sesame Workshop, www.sesameworkshop.org/aroundtheworld/kosovo
34 "Crackles of Hatred," *Economist*, July 25, 2009, 60.
35 Tom Coghlan, "Taliban Spin Doctors Winning Fresh Ground in Propaganda War with NATO," *The Times* (London), November 12, 2009.
36 Huda al Saleh, "Al Qaeda Continues Using Modern Technology To Recruit Youth," *Asharq Alawsat*, January 5, 2010.
37 Friedman, "America vs. the Narrative."
38 Joseph S. Nye, "How to Counter Terrorism's Online Generation," *Financial Times*, October 13, 2005.
39 Seth G. Jones and Martin C. Libicki, *How Terrorist Groups End* (Santa Monica, CA: RAND, 2008), xiii, xvii.
40 Jones and Libicki, *How Terrorist Groups End*, xvii.
41 Griff Witte, Jerry Markon, and Shaiq Hussain, "Terrorist Recruiters Leverage the Web," *Washington Post*, December 13, 2009.
42 Violent Islamist Extremism Al-Shabab Recruitment in America," United States Senate Hearing, March 11, 2009, http://hsgac.senate.gov/public/index.cfm?FuseAction=Hearings.Hearing_ID=35e68562-1606-409a-9118-3edfbb8e87c8
43 Steven Stalinsky, "Deleting Online Jihad and the Case of Anwar Al-Awlaki," MEMRI Inquiry and Analysis Series, no. 576, December 30, 2009.
44 Abdul Rahman Al-Rashed, "In Search of the Instructor in Yemen," *Asharq Alawsat*, December 29, 2009.

Selected bibiography

Books

Armstrong, Karen. *Muhammad: A Biography of the Prophet*. San Francisco: Harper-SanFrancisco, 1993.

Barnett, Brooke and Amy Reynolds. *Terrorism and the Press: An Uneasy Relationship*. New York: Peter Lang, 2009.

Bunt, Gary R. *Islam in the Digital Age*. London: Pluto Press, 2003.

Çapan, Ergün (Ed.). *Terror and Suicide Attacks: An Islamic Perspective*. New Jersey, NJ: The Light, 2005.

Corman, Steven R., Angela Trethewey, and H. L. Goodall, Jr. (eds.). *Weapons of Mass Persuasion: Strategic Communication To Combat violent Extremism*. New York: Peter Lang, 2008.

Dartnell, Michael Y. *Insurgency Online: Web Activism and Global Conflict*. Toronto, Canada: University of Toronto Press, 2006.

Devji, Faisal. *Landscapes of the Jihad*. Ithaca, NY: Cornell University Press, 2005.

Dobkin, Bethami A. *Tales of Terror: Television News and the Construction of the Terrorist Threat*. Westport, CT: Praeger, 1992.

Hoffman, Bruce. *Inside Terrorism*. New York: Columbia University Press, 1998.

Huntington, Samuel P. *The Clash of Civilizations and the Remaking of World Order*. New York: Simon and Schuster, 1996.

Jones, Seth G. and Martin C. Libicki. *How Terrorist Groups End*. Santa Monica, CA: RAND, 2008.

Kepel, Gilles. *Beyond Terror and Martyrdom*. Cambridge, MA: Belknap/Harvard, 2008.

———. *The War for Muslim Minds*. Cambridge, MA: Harvard University Press, 2006.

Kilcullen, David. *The Accidental Guerrilla: Fighting Small Wars in the midst of a Big One*. New York: Oxford University Press, 2009.

Langwith, Jacqueline (ed.). *Suicide: Opposing Viewpoints*.Greenhaven Press, 2008.

Lim, Merlyna. *Islamic Radicalism and Anti-Americanism in Indonesia: The Role of the Internet*. Washington, DC: East-West Center, 2005.

Martin, Gus (ed.). *The New Era of Terrorism: Selected Readings*. Thousand Oaks, CA: Sage, 2004.

Nacos, Brigitte L. *Mass-Mediated Terrorism* (2nd edition). Lanham, MD: Rowman and Littlefield, 2007.

National Commission on Terrorist Attacks. *The 9/11 Commission Report*. New York: W. W. Norton, 2004.

Pape, Robert. *Dying to Win: The Strategic Logic of Suicide Terrorism.* New York: Random House, 2005.

Pedahzur, Ami. *Root Causes of Suicide Terrorism: The Globalization of Martyrdom.* New York: Routledge, 2006.

Sageman, Marc. *Leaderless Jihad.* Philadelphia: University of Pennsylvania Press, 2008.

Schmid, Alex P. and Janny de Graaf. *Violence as Communication: Insurgent Terrorism and the Western News Media.* London: Sage Publications, 1982.

Seib, Philip. *The Al Jazeera Effect.* Dulles, VA: Potomac Books, 2008.

Skaine, Rosemarie. *Female Suicide Bombers.* Jefferson, NC: McFarland & Company, 2006.

Tuman, Joseph S. *Communicating Terror: The Rhetorical Dimensions of Terrorism* (2nd edition). Los Angeles: Sage, 2010.

Victor, Barbara. *Army of Roses: Inside the World of Palestinian Women Suicide Bombers.* New York: St. Martin's Press, 2003.

Weimann, Gabriel. *Terror on the Internet.* Washington, DC: United States Institute of Peace, 2006.

Wright, Lawrence. *The Looming Tower: Al Qaeda and the Road to 9/11.* New York: Knopf, 2006.

Articles, chapters, and reports

Abrahamian, Ervand. "The U.S. Media, Samuel Huntington, and September 11." *Middle East Report*, no. 223 (Summer 2002).

Arquilla, John, David Ronfeldt, and Michele Zanini. "Globally Wired: Politics in Cyberspace (Fourth in a Series): Information-Age Terrorism." *Current History*, 99, no. 636 (2000).

Baran, Zeyno. "Fighting the War of Ideas." *Foreign Affairs*, 84, no. 6.(2005).

Bergen, Peter. "Al Qaeda at 20, Dead or Alive?" *Washington Post*, August 17, 2008.

Coll, Steve and Susan B. Glasser. "Terrorists Move Operations to Cyberspace." *Washington Post*, August 7, 2005.

Conway, Maura. "Terrorism and the Internet." *Parliamentary Affairs*, 59, no. 2 (2006).

Dallal, Jenine Abboushi. "Hizballah's Virtual Civil Society." *Television and New Media*, 2, no. 4 (2001).

Geizhals, Rachel. "Social Media Users Successfully Face Down Nasrallah on Facebook." *Jerusalem Post*, July 29, 2009. www.jpost.com/servlet/Satellite?cid=1248277915968& pagename=JPArticle%2FShowFull

Getler, Michael. "The Language of Terrorism." *Washington Post*, September 21, 2003.

Glasser, Susan B. and Steve Coll. "The Web as Weapon." *Washington Post*, August 9, 2005.

Hoffman, Bruce. "The Use of the Internet by Islamic Extremists." Testimony presented to the House Permanent Select Committee on Intelligence, May, 2006.

Hosenball, Mark, Michael Isikoff, and Evan Thomas. "The Radicalization of Umar Farouk Abdulmutallab." *Newsweek*, January 2, 2010. www.newsweek.com/id/229047

Hoyt, Clark. "Separating the Terror and the Terrorists." *New York Times*, December 13, 2008.

Huntington, Samuel P. "The Clash of Civilizations?" *Foreign Affairs*, 72 (Summer 1993).

Hussain, Rashad and Al-Husein N. Madhany, "Reformulating the Battle of Ideas: Understanding the Role of Islam in Counterterrorism Policy." The Brookings Project on U.S. Relations with the Islamic World, Saban Center, the Brookings Institution, Analysis Paper no. 3, August 2008.

Ibish, Hussein and Anne Stewart. "Report on Hate Crimes and Discrimination Against Arab-Americans: The Post-September 11 Backlash." American-Arab Anti-Discrimination Committee (2003), www.adc.org/PDF/hcr02.pdf

Kahn, Jeremy. "Mumbai Terrorists Relied on New Technology for Attacks." *New York Times*, December 9, 2008. www.nytimes.com/2008/12/09/world/asia/09mumbai. html?pagewanted=print

Kifner, John. "Massacre Draws Self-Criticism in Muslim Press." *New York Times*, September 9, 2004.

Labi, Nadya. "Jihad 2.0." *Atlantic Monthly*, July/August 2006.

Lia, Brynjar. "Al Qaeda Online: Understanding Jihadist Internet Infrastructure." *Jane's Intelligence Review*, January 1, 2006.

———. "Al Qaeda's Appeal: Understanding Its Unique Selling Points." *Perspectives on Terrorism*, II, no. 8, May 2008.

Lieberman, Joseph and Susan Collins. "Violent Islamist Extremism, the Internet, and the Homegrown Terrorist Threat." *United States Senate Committee on Homeland Security and Governmental Affairs*, May 8, 2008. http://hsgac.senate.gov/public/ _files/IslamistReport.pdf

Lynch, Marc. "Al Qaeda's Media Strategies." *The National Interest*, Spring 2006.

Moss, Michael and Souad Mekhennet. "An Internet Jihad Aims at U.S. Viewers," *New York Times*, October 17, 2008, www.nytimes.com/2007/10/15/us/15net.html?_r= 1&oref=slogin

National Counterterrorism Center, *2008 Report on Terrorism*.

"One Year After the Summer War—Sixth Episode: Women of Hizballah." *Asharq Al-Awsat*, July 17, 2007. www.aawsat.com/details.asp?issueno=10458& article=428464

Riedel, Bruce. "Al Qaeda Strikes Back." *Foreign Affairs*, 86, no. 3, May/June 2007.

Rogan, Hanna. "Abu Reuter and the E-Jihad." *Georgetown Journal of International Affairs*, issue 8.2, Summer/Fall 2007.

———. "Jihadism Online." Forsvarets Forskninginstitutt, Norwegian Defense Research Establishment, FFI/Rapport2006/00915, March 2006.

Rubin, Alissa J. "Taliban Overhaul Image to Win Allies." *New York Times*, January 21, 2010.

Scheuer, Michael. "Al Qaeda's Media Doctrine: Evolution from Cheerleader to Opinion-Shaper." *Jamestown Foundation Terrorism Focus*, 4, no. 15, May 22, 2007.

Seib, Philip. "The News Media and the 'Clash of Civilizations.'" *Parameters*, XXIV, no. 4 (Winter 2004–05).

Silber, Mitchell D. and Arvin Bhatt. "Radicalization in the West: The Homegrown Threat." *The New York Police Department Intelligence Division* (2007). www.nypd-shield.org/public/SiteFiles/documents/NYPD_Report-Radicalization_in_the_West.pdf

Singer, Peter W. "Terrorists Must Be Denied Child Recruits." *Financial Times*, January 20, 2005.

Stenersen, Anne. "The Internet: A Virtual Training Camp?" *Terrorism and Political Violence*, 20 (2008).

Swartz, Jon. "Terrorists' Use of Internet Spreads." *USA Today*, February 21, 2005.

"Sympathizers Seek Answers from Al-Qaida: Questions to al-Zawahri for 'On-line Interview' Unanswered So Far." *The Associated Press*, January 21, 2008. www. msnbc.msn.com/id/22767244/from/ET/

Tsfati, Yariv and Gabriel Weimann. "www.terrorism.com: Terror on the Internet." *Studies in Conflict and Terrorism*, 25, no. 5 (2002).

"Umar Farouk Abdulmutallab: One Boy's Journey to Jihad." *TimesOnline*, January 3, 2010. www.timesonline.co.uk/tol/news/world/middle_east/article6974073.ece

United States Senate Committee on homeland Security and Governmental Affairs, "Violent Islamist Extremism, the Internet, and the Homegrown Terrorist Threat." May 8, 2008.

Weimann, Gabriel. "Virtual disputes: The Use of the Internet for Terrorist Debates," *Studies in Conflicts and Terrorism*, 29, no. 7 (2006).

———. "www.terror.net: How Modern Terrorism Uses the Internet." Washington, DC: United States Institute of Peace (2004). www.usip.org/pubs/specialreports/sr116.pdf

Whitlock, Craig. "Al Qaeda's Growing Online Offensive." *Washington Post*, June 24, 2008.

———. "The New Al Qaeda Central." *Washington Post*, September 9, 2007.

"Who is Anwar al-Awlaki?" *The Week*, January 4, 2009. www.theweek.com/article/index/102685/Who_is_Anwar_alAwlaki

"Winning or Losing: A Special Report on Al Qaeda." *Economist*, July 19, 2008.

Wolfowitz, Paul. "Prepared Statement for the House Armed Services Committee." Washington, DC, August 10 (2004). www.defenselink.mil/speeches/speech.aspx?speechid=143

Younis, Noora. "'Al-Masry Al-Yawm' Reveals Pictures: Palestinian Women Join the 'Heart' of the Resistance." *Al-Masry Al-Youm*, March 16, 2009. www.almasry-alyoum.com/article2.aspx?ArticleID=203046& IssueID=1346

Index

138   *Index*

Guantanamo prison 89
Gulf War 12

Habermasian 43
Halliburton 32
Hamas 3, 5, 9, 28–29, 49, 68, 70–73, 80,
   94, 108, 110, 113
Hezbollah 3, 28–29, 34, 57, 68–71, 76,
   85, 93–94, 108
hijab 16
Holsti's six basic elements 44–57
homegrown terrorism 3, 28, 62, 90, 91,
   117
Huntington, Samuel 11–12, 44
Hussein, Saddam 12, 18

Idris, Wafa 79, 86, 94
interactivity 54, 56, 59, 62, 89, 91
Internet; terrorists' message 45–46, 59;
   finance 55
Internet security 27, 31–33, 37, 53, 55,
   59–60, 64, 104–5
Iraq War 14, 34, 43, 45, 82
Irhabi 007 82
Islamic Army in Iraq 49, 59, 77, 87
Islamic Front for the Iraqi Resistance
   48–49, 51, 54, 56
Islamic Resistance Movement 48–49,
   53–55

Jamaat Ansar Al-Sunna 49
Jamiyyat Ul Islam Is Saheeh 90
Japanese Kamikaze pilots 47
Jaradat, Hanadi 76, 86
Jewish Internet Defense Force 94
Jihad and Change Front 46, 57
Jihad and Tawhid Forum 52, 56
Jihad on the Land of Rafedean Brigades
   48, 82
Jihadization 91

Khaled, Amr 16
Kohlmann, Evan 48
Kurdistan Workers' Party 76

Lamar James, Kevin 90
language on the Internet 49, differences
   56
Lockheed Martin 46

Madrid train bombings 10, 22, 90,
magazines 26–27, 29, 34, 48–49, 53–54,
   70, 114
Mahdi Army 51

Marshall, Paul 46
martyrs 9, 11, 20, 25, 50, 68–69, 71–72,
   78–82, 83, 85–86, 98; on Internet 11,
   16–19, 22, 24–36, 38, 43–68, 77–78,
   82, 88–100, 102–4, 109–12
Martyrs Foundation 81
McVeigh, Timothy 2
Mideast Youth 64–66, 111
mothers of martyrs 81
multimedia 11, 18, 26, 29–33, 49–52, 58;
   educating users 52, 60; video 33–36,
   38–40, 42, 46–48, 50–54, 59–62, 66,
   86, 92, 94, 96, 99, 115
Mumbai attacks 8, 19, 54
Muslim Brotherhood 15, 73, 110

Nablus Province Police Department 77
Nasrallah, Hassan 28, 94
Nationalist and Islamic Front 49, 82
Netanyahu, Binyamin 5
news media 1, 3, 6–10, 11–18, 25, 31,
   36, 48–50, 58, 74, 93, 101
Northern Ireland 5, 113

Oklahoma City 3
Omar, Fatima 83
online forums 15, 19–20, 26, 31–33,
   36–37, 54–56, 62, 64, 69, 77, 82–86,
   89, 92–93, 97–99, 110

Patriot Act 58
Pearl, Daniel 19, 55
PFLF-GC 48–50, 52, 56
Popular Front for the Liberation of
   Palestine 46–47, 81
post-Cold War era 12, 14
poster competitions 53
Protect America Act 58

radicalization 3, 19–20, 60, 62, 67,
   89–91

Saraya Al-Quds 77, 78, 86, 94
Schmid and de Graaf 44
Shin Bet 93
Sister Harb 82–83
State Department's Office of the
   Coordinator for Counterterrorism 44
suicide attacks 47–48, 56, 66, 75–76,
   79–81, 85, 87–88, 98

Tamil Tigers 66, 76
Tawhid and Jihad Forum 49, 53
Twitter 62, 63, 69, 95–96, 112, 115

CPSIA information can be obtained
at www.ICGtesting.com
Printed in the USA
FSOW02n1042291214
4207FS

9 780415 779623